at the Institute of Education, The University of Leeds, under the Directorship of Joan Tough, and with the help of Elizabeth Rainsbury, then Principal Lecturer in Education at Ripon College, and Eunice Bailey, Warden of the University of Leeds Children's Centre, and four groups of teachers. The approach which was developed was based on the evidence of a longitudinal study of children's use of language which had been carried out by Joan Tough over a period of years.

The Schools Council's feasibility study led to the establishment of the Communication Skills in Early Childhood Project, with funds of approximately £75,000. Later an additional grant of £14,000 was made available in order to extend the Project to help teachers of young children who are learning to use English as a second language. During the years 1973 to 1976 the Project was accommodated in the University of Leeds Institute of Education. With the cooperation of some 90 groups of teachers throughout England, Wales and Northern Ireland, and the help of advisers and of wardens of teachers centres in many local authorities, a cooperative effort began in designing materials to help teachers develop insight, and the necessary skills.

Listening to Children Talking: A Guide to the Appraisal of Children's Use of Language and its companion volume *Talking and Learning: A Guide to Fostering Communication Skills in Nursery and Infant Schools*, embody aims, methods and techniques which have been found to be effective and practical in classroom application.

Although the books are concerned with the kind of education that is appropriate for all young children, we have always in mind the particular needs of those children who are at disadvantage within school because of their experiences of using language at home.

What can be done in school to foster the development of communication skills in all young children, but most importantly, in those for whom school may provide the only experiences which will extend their skills of thinking and using language?

If the teacher is to be able to give the most effective help to all the children in her care, it follows that somehow a way must be found of gaining a view of each child's ability in using language

and so discovering what his problems seem to be. The main purpose of *Listening to Children Talking* is to help teachers to make an appraisal of children's skill in using language as they listen to them talking, and as they talk with them, helping them to explore ideas and experiences.

Before we can usefully discuss what the teacher can do, however, it seems necessary to consider what the child might be expected to have learned about using language in the years before he comes to school, and the reasons for the differences that are seen between children, and that all teachers of young children know exist. The first part of this book discusses the way in which children develop language, and considers some of the reasons for the differences which we find between children when they come to nursery or infant school. The second part considers some of the problems that young children have in using speech, problems that hinder their efforts to communicate. The aim of the last part of the book is to help teachers identify a range of uses of language as they talk with children. This will enable them to discover what the child has already learned, and decide on the kind of help he needs.

The second volume *Talking and Learning: A Guide to Fostering Communication Skills in Nursery and Infant Schools* will then go on to examine ways in which the teacher might promote the development of the child's skills in using language: skills that will contribute to the quality of his learning and enable him to examine his experiences more effectively.

The guides have been designed so that they might be useful to the teacher who reads and follows the suggestions for classroom practice, building up skills gradually. But the books will serve teachers more usefully when they are used as a basis for group discussion and workshop sessions, organized within schools or within teachers centres, or wherever teachers meet together to consider the knowledge and skills of their profession. Taken in conjunction with the suggested activities of observing and listening to children talking and developing skills of analysis and interaction, the books are seen as a means of stimulating a programme which explores the principles which should underlie practice, and leads to mutual help amongst teachers who are wanting to develop these new skills.

For those who wish to use the guides with groups of teachers, a series of video tapes has been made to introduce each of the topics which are dealt with in the two books. The video tapes offer examples of children using language and of teachers and children talking together, which not only provide material for discussion and critical analysis, but also provide illustrations of a range of uses of language, of strategies for interaction, and the problems children and teachers encounter when they talk together. Suggestions for the organization of workshop sessions, using the guides and video tapes, are outlined in a booklet *Communication Skills Workshop*. Courses for leaders of such study groups are held regularly at the University of Leeds School of Education, and may be held from time to time at other centres.

Suggestions for practical work in the classroom, books for further reading and questions for discussion with colleagues are provided at appropriate points in the book. Some notes on how this book might be used to provide the basis for workshop discussions between colleagues in school will be found on pp. 128 and 129 in appendix one.

Teachers working with the Project have found that workshop sessions provide valuable experience for, in working together, they have found new depths of understanding of children's learning and a new awareness of their own role in the process. Together they have built new resources of knowledge and skills that have brought new meaning to education in early childhood, not only for the children but also for themselves as educators.

We should point out, however, that the insights to be gained and the new skills to be developed are not easily won, and those who wish to acquire them will need to be willing to examine their own attitudes and practices carefully and critically, and be prepared to sustain their efforts to establish new skills over a considerable period. The teachers who have helped to fashion these materials have acknowledged the value of working in this way, and claim to have gained both personally and professionally from it. Whether teachers work alone from this guide, or work with others, we hope that they too will gain satisfaction from their increased understanding of children's problems in using language, and their own increasing skill in appraising what children *do* with language.

References

PARRY, M. (1975) *Preschool Education* (Schools Council Research Studies) Macmillan

PARRY, M. and ARCHER, H. (1975) *Two to Five* (Schools Council Preschool Education Project (2–5)) Macmillan

SCHOOLS COUNCIL COMMUNICATION
SKILLS IN EARLY CHILDHOOD PROJECT

LISTENING TO CHILDREN TALKING:

A guide to the appraisal of children's
use of language

Joan Tough

S WARD LOCK EDUCATIONAL
in association with
DRAKE EDUCATIONAL ASSOCIATES

Project Team members

Director	Dr Joan Tough
Project Officers	Dorothea Bennett
	Mary Jane Drummond
	Elizabeth Sestini
Assistant Project Officer 1973–5	Nicola Coupe
Research Assistant	Lois Garling
Research Fellow	Asra Treisman
Teacher Fellows (one year appointments)	
1973–4	Jill Hancock
1974–5	Jeanne Forster
	Sheila Nightingale
	Val Reid
1975–6	Jean Hepworth
	Joyce Jurica

Illustrations by Sylvia Deakins

ISBN 0 7062 3506 1 paperback
     0 7062 3507 X hardback

First published 1976
Reprinted 1976

Set in 10 on 12 Monotype Plantin
by Woolaston Parker Limited, Leicester
and printed by Robert MacLehose and Company Limited
for Ward Lock Educational
116 Baker Street, London W1M 2BB and
Drake Educational Associates
212 Whitchurch Road, Cardiff CF4 3XF
Made in Great Britain

This book is to be returned on or before
the last date stamped below.

Communication Skills in Early Childhood Project materials

Listening to Children Talking: A Guide to the Appraisal of Children's Use of language (175 pages; available in paperback and hardback)
Two sets of picture charts to accompany the above book:
Set 1 Black kitten gets lost
Set 2 Dad forgets his dinner

Communications Skills Workshop (Stage 1 Appraisal)
(See page 175 for details)
6 videotapes
Workshop Leader's Handbook
Workshop Members' Worksheets

Publication spring 1977
Talking and Learning: A Guide to Fostering Communication Skills in Nursery and Infant Schools (160 pages approx; available in paperback and hardback)
Communications Skills Workshop (Stage 2 Fostering)
(Details to be announced)
6 videotapes
Workshop Leader's Handbook
Workshop Members' Worksheets

CONTENTS

Preface

This *Guide to the Appraisal of Children's Use of Language* is the first publication to be produced by the Schools Council's Project on Communication Skills in Early Childhood. The methods outlined in this book have been formulated and tested with the help of some 1,500 nursery and infant teachers working in groups in many parts of the country. May we here extend our thanks to them all, for without doubt, the materials which have evolved must be more relevant to teachers' needs, and of more practical use in the classroom, than ever they could have been without their help.

The Project arose directly from the experiences of the Preschool Education Project, the first Schools Council project to be concerned with the education of children below statutory school age. In the first project Marianne Parry and Hilda Archer surveyed and recorded, with the help of many teachers in nursery schools and classes, those experiences which were being offered to young children which might be considered to be the best of present practice in nursery education. This work has been described in two books, *Preschool Education* (Parry 1975) and *Two to Five* (Parry and Archer 1975).

From the survey came evidence of the kind of guidance and help that teachers of young children felt was needed. An important area in which teachers showed a great deal of interest, but also an awareness of their own lack of knowledge, was the development and use of language and the contribution that teachers could make to the development of young children's skills in communicating.

At the time of this first project there was considerable interest developing in the problems of disadvantage and of the association, demonstrated by research, between educational achievement, disadvantage, and skill in using language. Reports were coming from the USA about curricula which were being developed under the Headstart Policy in an effort to recognize and offset the disadvantage of many children from the poor sections of the community when they first came to school. Marianne Parry and Hilda Archer expressed concern about the approaches that many of these curricula were taking, with their emphasis on language tests, the repetition of linguistic patterns reminiscent of second-language teaching to older pupils, and their use of kits of teaching aids. Most infant and nursery teachers in this country see such approaches as inappropriate for the early stages of learning, since they neglect several dimensions of learning that traditionally teachers of young children in this country hold to be important, particularly that of developing an impetus towards learning that stems from the child's own interests and activities.

The Preschool Education Project recognized that teachers need more knowledge about the characteristics of disadvantage in early childhood, particularly about children's early learning in the home, and the role of the language experience in the learning process. It called for an examination of alternative approaches to the promotion of language skills in young children in school and appealed for help for teachers, so that they might develop skill in recognizing children's problems in using language. It recognized the need for developing strategies for the deliberate stimulation of language skills in contexts which were more compatible with our knowledge of development and learning in the early years, and with our traditional approaches to early childhood education.

The Project on Communication Skills in Early Childhood represents, then, an effort to meet the needs which the Preschool Education Project had identified. With a grant of £8,000 from Schools Council a feasibility study was established in 1971

PART ONE

Learning to use language:
the years before school

Chapter one

Language and learning in early childhood

Language and communication

All teachers would probably agree that language not only plays an important part in the social and intellectual development of young children, but that it provides for everyone, adult and child alike, the most generally effective means of communication. Until the child can express his ideas, intentions and needs through the use of language, other people can only guess what it is he wants them to know from his gestures and actions, from the tone of his voice and from his facial expression.

Some would argue that language is only one means of communication available to the child, and this clearly is true. But sometimes perhaps we use the term *communication* to refer to incidents in which communication does not take place. Often the adult, parent or teacher, anticipates what the child is wanting or intends, because his problem, his likes and dislikes, and the signs of his different moods, are so well known. Thus, if we see a child sitting despondently in a corner, with drooping shoulders and puckered brow, we take these as signs that all is not well with him. We begin to guess the likely cause of his dejection from what we know about him as a person and from what we know about the relationships he has with other children, and also from what we know about his recent experiences at home or in school. Often we say that the child is communicating to us something of his feelings through his general demeanour, but perhaps it is rather that we are recognizing symptoms in his behaviour and drawing conclusions about the likely causes. Sometimes we also discover that we have considerably misinterpreted what we have seen from what he says, or does, sometime later.

Often teachers use the term *communication* when referring to activities other than those which depend on language. For example we frequently refer to children's paintings or drawings, or efforts in dramatic movement or modern dance, or music, as providing a means of communication. While we can see that much activity may express some of the child's ideas, and that the spectator may make some interpretation of what he sees or hears, there may be little relationship between the child's intentions and the spectator's interpretation. There may be the essence of communication in modern movement or dance, where each of the participants responds to the other, anticipating mood and intention and shaping the response accordingly, and the same may be the case in spontaneous music making. But in talking about *communication* in this book, we are regarding the intention to pass some information to another, and the readiness to receive the intended message, as necessary conditions for communication to take place. The effectiveness of any medium used for communication then, would be the extent to which the message which was intended by the one, coincided with the information received by the other. If we take this as our definition of communication then we can see that other media, which we often think of as offering a means of communication, may not be effective for this purpose. There may be the expression of ideas on the part of one person, and an interpretation on the part of another, but until the ideas are also expressed through language, we cannot know how effective communication has been.

It is true that some highly stylised forms—cartoons and mime for example—can express an intended message that will be interpreted correctly by everyone. But there is a limit to the kind of message that can be effectively given in this form. It is also true that communication can take place through gesture or action—the hand squeezed in sympathy for example—but again, for the meaning to be made clear, language becomes necessary.

Language, we would hold, provides the most effective means of communication, but this is not to say that we are always successful in communicating when we use language. There is frequently great misunderstanding between the child and the adult, and often between adult and adult, but we can see that language provides us with the means of trying to make our meanings clear and to dispel misunderstanding. Skill in communicating, then, is concerned with establishing ways of expressing and interpreting information, ideas or meanings so effectively that misunderstanding is avoided.

The importance of language

We do not need to justify the importance we attach to helping children develop language in nursery and infant schools: it is clearly important for the child and teacher to be able to communicate, to tell each other what they are thinking and feeling, and to give and receive directions and information. Nor should we feel that to be concerned with language is inappropriate because of the child's stage of development. Quite basic to the child's development of language is his urgent need to communicate, to gain the attention of others, particularly of adults, to inform them of his needs and wishes. From this comes the driving force, the motivation for the child to persist in trying to master language and use it for his own ends.

But using language has other implications: it is not just that being able to communicate is important, we must consider the importance of what is being communicated, and particularly the importance of that which can *only* be communicated by using language. There is a good deal of evidence which suggests that language may fulfil important functions besides that of enabling communication to take place, and we will consider it briefly at this point.

The first and most important aspect is that the development of language may play an important part in the child's intellectual or cognitive development. Some of the most striking evidence here comes from work carried out by Vygotsky in the Soviet Union some forty years ago, work which was not known in this country until much later. In *Thought and Language* Vygotsky describes a number of experiments which support his conclusion that as the child learns to use words so he is helped to develop concepts, that is ideas about objects and events as they exist, and the relationships which can be seen to exist between them.

Vygotsky shows that each time a particular word is used the child's attention is drawn to one more instance of the concept so that in time the word comes to represent a general idea which has developed from many experiences. For example the word 'dog' may be at first be understood only as referring to a particular dog—the family pet, or the dog next door, or perhaps one seen in a book or on television. But as the word 'dog' is used each time another dog is met in the streets, on visits to friends, in the pet shop perhaps, the child sees many examples of dog and hears them all referred to by the word 'dog'. In fact the animals to which the name 'dog' is given may differ greatly from one another—they will range in size from very small to very large, they will be of many colours and shapes. As the child generalizes the use of the term to include all dogs he may at first include all four-legged animals. But as he hears other words associated with some of these animals, he gradually begins to pick out all the essential features which dogs have in common and distinguish them from other four-legged creatures. So as he builds up other general notions from many instances, we can see that by hearing words used as labels for objects and actions he is gradually being helped to delineate many concepts. Thus he comes to know, for example, which features to look for in deciding whether an animal he meets belongs to those which are labelled 'dog' or those which are labelled 'cat' and later he will learn that both cats and dogs are included as 'animals'.

We can see that as the child hears and uses words he is being helped to see some kind of order in what he is experiencing, and he is able to recognize those instances which have some basic qualities in common. In this way the use of language helps the child to begin to classify objects, actions and situations which make up his experiences.

As soon as the child has established a few words for common objects or situations, he begins to test as it were their meaning, almost as though he were hypothesizing about the meaning of a word. Thus his own efforts set up conditions in which new words are offered to him. For example, the child usually establishes a word which refers to the drinks he is offered, and will use it to demand drinks from bottles, jugs, and cups. Does 'drink' encompass the whole of the situation? Sometimes he will point to a cup or jug and utter the word 'drink'. The rejoinder will often make clear that the drink is the stuff that goes into the container and that the words 'cup' or 'bottle' refer to special kinds of containers. Thus trying to use words and making a 'mistake' often means that the child draws help to himself, and he is helped to make new distinctions.

The dimensions of experience

Many concepts can be derived directly from what we often refer to as concrete experience. The child who bumps his head on the table can understand the hardness he will meet when he comes into contact with the table. Knowing the word 'hard' does not, perhaps, add any more to his understanding of the attribute hard, but it certainly makes it possible for him to communicate about this quality. Much of the evidence from the development of concepts by deaf children shows that it is possible for many concepts to be developed directly from concrete experience and without the help of language. This evidence is described in Furth's *Thinking Without Language* and in Lewis's *Language and Personality in Deaf Children*. But Vygotsky holds that there are many concepts which are not readily recognized from experience—those which refer to qualities and relationships for example—and for these the child's learning will be more dependent upon the adult, who helps the child gradually through talking and explaining to come to understand and develop abstract ideas. Until the child can read for himself

and respond to the written words, he must depend on adults (or older children who have established these skills), for gaining new information and extending his thinking to abstract ideas. As adults talk with him about his experiences, offer new experiences to him and discuss them with him, so he gains new meaning for familiar experiences and is helped to build up those concepts about the world which cannot be abstracted readily from immediate concrete experience.

The organizing function of language

In Vygotsky's view, then, language plays a critical part in conceptual development. But there are those, like Piaget and his colleagues in Geneva, who would stress that the child's thinking stems from his own actions and that it is through the information that his senses provide, and from the information which he gains about objects and events through his own actions upon them, that the child is able to set up inside himself a model of the world around him to which he is able to refer as he considers the problems which are confronting him and seeks to understand new experiences. In this view, sensory experiences and the child's increasing maturity are the important factors in the child's development of concepts. Language is held to be important because it increases the range and rapidity of thought, as Inhelder and Piaget comment in *The Early Growth of Logic in the Child*, because using language gives us the means of making quick reference to, say, a series of actions or to something which is a complex structure. To be able to say, for example, 'I am going to get a builder to build me a house' takes a very short time to communicate because, in using language, we have drawn on vocabulary and sentence structure in both of which is embedded a range of very complex agreed meanings. Without language to 'hold' complex meanings of this kind it would become very difficult to demonstrate the characteristics of *house*, or the sequences of *building*, or the skills necessary for a man to be called *a builder*. Because language has possibilities for making references in this way and meaning can be changed by very small differences in the arrangement of words or by small additions or deletions, the message can be short but hold complex meaning.

We can see, then, that language allows complex meanings to be expressed with great economy and frees the child's thinking from dependence upon the presence of objects and materials. He can refer to experiences long past or look forward to events which have not yet happened. Without language, communication of this kind is not possible and therefore it can, with justification, be said that language frees thinking and communication from the restrictions of the concrete present. Language helps us to organize information that we want to convey into manageable and economic expression.

The child's thinking is not like the adult's, however, so that even where he has developed considerable knowledge about language, the kind of thinking he will express will be restricted by his own level of understanding. This, Piaget and his colleagues have made very clear in numerous experiments which look at different aspects of the child's thinking. Many experiments have shown that the child's thinking is dependent on the development of his inner frames of reference, which have been built from his own perceptions and actions.

The language experience

The discussion so far may suggest that the views of Vygotsky and Piaget are in some conflict and they are often presented in this light by others, but it seems that both can be seen as perfectly valid views of the phenomenon of language and the part it is playing in the child's development.

We can agree with Piaget that the child's experiences provide the basis from which meaning, and so language, can develop. At the same time we can accept Vygotsky's view that as others use language with the child, what they say plays a part in stimulating the child's actions and setting value on them. So if someone says to him, 'Look at the bee in the centre of the daisy there', the child's attention may be drawn not only to the flower and the bee, so that he looks at them more closely, but also to the fact that it is a good thing to look for interesting details in the world around him. With

his attention focussed in this way, he may be provoked to make comparisons with previous experiences and note differences, or to ask questions and seek further information. The very act of using language to draw attention to what the adult finds significant and meaningful, is to help the child to look at the world around him with a particular perspective, as well as encouraging alertness and stimulating curiosity and interest. It seems likely that in families where parents and brothers and sisters have interests which they share with the child, the child will learn not only something about the topics which form the basis for discussion, but at the same time he is also likely to adopt attitudes which are displayed by others towards people, towards natural phenomena, towards the happenings in the neighbourhood, towards the use of books and instruments. What is shown to be worthwhile is likely to become worthwhile to the child also, and the purposes for which others around him use language are likely to become the uses of language which he himself will employ.

The directive function of language

Another important use of language is concerned with the speaker's own actions. In an interesting series of experiments, Luria, another Soviet psychologist, has shown how language serves to help the young child direct and control his own actions. Even in adulthood we often use language in a self-directive capacity to control, or pace, our actions. When we are learning an intricate sequence of actions—learning to knit, drive a car, or use some tool or instrument—we are likely not only to monitor the sequence of actions, but also to anticipate and direct the fingers to carry out actions. Language used in this way seems to serve as the coordinator or regulator of action. As the young child talks to himself, and indeed as the adult talks to himself, it is almost as though it helps to bring action under control, so that the sequence is learned and becomes familiar, until the point when the actions are so well rehearsed and automatic that the use of directive language is no longer needed.

So we can see that these several dimensions of

language experience exist side by side and play an important part in the child's development. The language the child has developed serves as a means of communicating about his thinking and of directing his own and other people's actions; at the same time the language used by others with him helps him to find order, significance and meaning in the world around him, and to establish values for different activities and experiences.

Language and relationships: some differences in children's learning

There is another dimension of the language experience which has a pervasive and important effect on the purposes for which the child will come to use language. As we use language with one another we are, sometimes consciously but more often without awareness of what we do, indicating the kind of relationship which we assume exists between ourselves and the person spoken to. It is in this area of the kind of relationships that children have with others, particularly those they have with adults, that there may be very important differences in their experiences which will result in differences between children, not only in the way in which they view other people, but also the way in which they will view the world in general. This dimension of experience may be most important in accounting for differences between children in what is learned during the early years at home.

As we watch children playing and engaging in everyday activities we can see that there are many experiences that they will have in common. All children learn through their actions. Physical environments can be very different, but all children are likely to discover that some things are more resistant than others; for example, they all scrape their knees and bang their heads, and they are all likely to come to recognize colours and shapes and to deal with the spatial aspects of their environments and develop a concept of time. It is true that the kind of surroundings that they live in will be vastly different. There are, for example, wide differences between rural and urban environments and the persisting qualities of their environments will build

different expectations. Nevertheless, most children from cities will come to recognize farm animals, trees and fields, and children from the country will come to understand the problem of crossing busy roads.

So we can assume that children hold experiences in common from which everyday concepts can be built, although there will be differences between children in the specific knowledge they have built up from living in particular environments. The greatest differences in the experiences between children are likely to be those that stem from the particular expectations of life within their own families. All children learn to get along with others around them, and adjust to some extent to what is expected of them, in order to fulfil their need for acceptance and to gain love and recognition. But what is expected of them may be very different and so what they learn is different. Attitudes and values are implicit in the way in which language is used within the family and are for the most part never examined. The users are not aware that the way in which they talk with one another is reinforcing attitudes and relationships: their use of language reflects their way of life.

Much research has now examined the kind of differences that are apparent in the way in which children use language which may be attributed to the way of life and to the purpose for which language is used in the home. In this country the work done by Bernstein and his colleagues was the first in the field. This work is fully reported in the two volumes of *Class, Codes and Control*. There is now so much confirmatory evidence that we perhaps would no longer question the fact that there will be differences between children in the way in which they use language which stem from their experiences in the social environment of their homes.

A great deal of work has been undertaken in America also, and differences in the use of language have been found between children from different sections of the population. The problems spring not only from the class structure of society, but also from what is inextricably bound up in it, the problems of a multicultural population in which economic equality between different cultural groups clearly does not exist.

Early learning experiences and progress in school

There has been a great deal of confusion over the kind of language experiences that are related to the progress children make in school and consequently to the approaches to be adopted for meeting children's needs. We will not go into the details of the research here, but in the wake of the findings, both in this country and in the United States, has come a reaction which might have been anticipated. On the one hand there are those who attribute learning problems to lack of appropriate vocabulary and syntax. This interpretation has led others to question whether it matters that people use language differently: who is to say that one way should be more highly valued than another? A movement has now developed which claims that differences in the use of language are irrelevant and which seeks to end discrimination, including reaction to the way in which people speak. If the differences could be shown to lie only in speech forms and manner of talking such a view might be justified.

On the other hand, there are those who see the differences that are apparent as a reflection of basic attitudes which influence the way in which children come to interpret their experiences. If the differences in the way in which language is used are in some way contributing to differences in the way in which children learn, then this could account, at least in part, for the link that has been demonstrated between educational achievement and social class. Studies of the development of the use of language in young children and of the effects of differences in their experiences, which stem from the quality of the relationship that the child has with his mother and the way in which talk is used between them, have explored this possibility.

There have been several attempts in this country to gain a view of how, and for what purposes, the mother engages the child in talk. For the most part these studies have been based on what mothers have said they do with their children. Differences have emerged between what middle-class and working-class mothers report they talk about to their children. It is not easy to record representative samples of mothers and children talking together at home in order to investigate this aspect further. Some discussion of the results of a study of the language used by young children is provided in the next chapter, and in chapter three we will discuss the importance of the way in which mothers use language with their children.

The findings from research of this kind can be expected to be controversial and to raise debate about the inferences that can justifiably be drawn. There are implicit values which lie behind this kind of research and since findings might influence social and educational policies it tends to become a sensitive area for discussion. Do children who are at educational disadvantage because of their experiences at home need a special kind of education? Should emphasis be placed on educating mothers or their children? Is it just in the area of using language that mothers and children need help, or is the problem of wider significance? Much of the difficulty of identifying the causes of educational disadvantage stems from the nature of language itself. To examine the way in which language is being used it is necessary to find samples of language being used: this means collecting children's talk in some kind of situation which can be seen to be revealing the important aspects of language use. Yet this kind of data is particularly difficult to analyse. The tendency is to fall back on aspects of speech structure, syntax and vocabulary, yet many would argue that these do not necessarily reflect the purposes which language is serving. The report by Joan Tough on a longitudinal study of children's language *The Development of Meaning: A Study of Children's Use of Language* discusses problems of this kind more fully. This study shows how misleading results which are drawn from a study of linguistic features might be, and reflects upon the superficiality which stems from looking to the improvement of a child's use of language by trying to teach him patterns and forms of speech, instead of looking to the child's natural motivation for learning to use language.

During recent years, then, a body of evidence has grown which seems to indicate that the way in which the child learns to use language is dependent upon his early experiences in the home. Since those experiences are not likely to change in character throughout his childhood, the language of his home will provide a reinforcing background from his early learning, even though he meets new influences in his peer group and in school.

In later chapters we shall consider what it is that children can learn to do with language and what it is in their early experiences which seems to be so crucial. We will now consider some of the efforts that have been made to meet the needs of children who are at educational disadvantage.

Some educational strategies to improve children's use of language

In the United States many experimental programmes have been tried out with groups of young children and gains have been recorded in the young children with whom they have been used. Some of these programmes have also been tried in this country.

The majority of the experimental programmes so far produced originated as part of the Headstart Policy in the USA, which was concerned with helping disadvantaged children, particularly from ethnic minorities, to be better prepared for the work in school. It was conceived as trying to make good the accumulated deficit in learning that some children were believed to have. Their problems were considered to result from deficiency in particular linguistic skills and the earliest programmes were designed to give children practice in those skills.

Some approaches reflected the view that disadvantaged children would benefit most from rote learning. Thus routines were prepared in which the teacher engaged the child in a repetition of particular linguistic structures. A climate of competition and reward of effort was to be built up so that the child was motivated to try to give 'right' answers.

Other assumptions underlying some programmes were that the disadvantaged child fares badly in school either because he is rejected by the teacher and so robbed of confidence in his own ability to succeed, or because the teacher has not the skills which are needed for teaching him. Some programmes were designed to offset the teacher's lack of skills, by providing the basic teaching materials and the models from which children were to learn.

Some programmes were designed to operate in a climate of fun, so that the children gained confidence in their ability to answer, and found learning enjoyable and so looked forward to the next session. The *Peabody Language Development Kit* is the best example in this country of this fun-based provision, which generally uses second-language teaching techniques.

In the view of many, these programmes fail to tackle the basic problems which some children have. Language is not best seen as a set of skills to be established by drilling; this is to neglect the essential character of language which is its potential for expressing meaning. For the child to learn to use language successfully he needs to have strong motivation for wanting to express his own ideas. Language is a means of self-expression as well as of communication. Essentially the child needs to be motivated to examine his own experiences and to express what he sees as meaningful, and to be helped to see the possibility for meaning in his experiences, if he is to develop attitudes which will promote his learning even when the teacher is not working with him directly. The materials of the programmed language kits may hold his attention, and give him practice in using particular linguistic structures, but there seems to be little to suggest that it will carry over into other learning. All the evidence so far is that though the children become better at giving the kind of responses which are practised, this does not benefit them much when they come to school; that is, the programmes have not developed skills which help them to meet the expectations of school.

Other approaches which are seen to help the child to respond more effectively to his early school experiences are based on learning through the intrinsic motivation provided by play and the child's curiosity. The British nursery school and nursery class are perhaps the most notable exponents of this approach. Although we are convinced of the soundness of this approach, there is still little direct evidence to show whether or not it is effective in promoting communication skills. We need to reconsider the role that language plays in early education and recognize that as the child is learning to use language he is also learning basic attitudes to the world around him, to the people and events within it, and towards learning itself. We should be building on the intrinsic motivation to use language which develops as the child talks with others and finds new meaning in his experiences and new understanding for what is happening around him. But this hardly seems likely to happen where the child is seen as passively learning the structures of language and his main incentive to learn is praise from the teacher. The use of language is not likely to become more than knowing prescribed answers under these circumstances, and when the teacher is not there to listen and praise, it seems possible that the child will feel little need to use these skills.

We need to understand why children develop such different skills in using language. What is it about the child's early learning experiences that can have so important an effect upon the way in which he is able to use language when he comes to school? What accounts for the wide differences between children's ability to use language as an effective means of communication? If we can understand the problems that place children at disadvantage in school, then perhaps we can find more effective means of helping them; means which will seek to develop an impetus within the child to use language

as a tool for examining and extending the meaning of his own experiences, which will lead to the development of skills of thinking and of communicating which will provide both a basis and the means for his early education.

References

BERNSTEIN, B. (1971) *Class, Codes and Control Volumes 1 and 2* Routledge and Kegan Paul

FURTH, H. G. (1966) *Thinking without Language* Collier-Macmillan

INHELDER, B. and PIAGET, J. (1964) *The Early Growth of Logic in the Child* Routledge and Kegan Paul

LEWIS, M. M. (1968) *Language and Personality in Deaf Children* NFER

PEABODY LANGUAGE DEVELOPMENT KIT (1968) Dunn, Morton and Smith

LURIA, A. R. (1961) *The Role of Speech in the Regulation of Normal and Abnormal Behaviour* Pergamon

TOUGH, J. (1977) *The Development of Meaning: A Study of Children's Use of Language* Allen and Unwin

VYGOTSKY, L. S. (1962) *Thought and Language* New York: Wiley

Chapter two

The development of language

Children's potential for using language

When the child comes to school, whether at the age of three or four or five, it is clear that he is not a beginner in learning to use language. Most four and five year olds, and many three year olds, show that they have already mastered much of the intricacy of using speech, and demonstrate their understanding of the purposes which language serves as they express their needs, wishes and ideas, and respond to the talk of other people.

The child of three has been a speaker for a relatively short time, but we must suppose that in the ordinary way he experiences so much language used around him and with him, that he is given more than enough practice in distinguishing the things to which words refer, and the particular meaning which is expressed by the way in which words are ordered. At three and four he will still be making many mistakes, but gradually he overcomes them so that by six or seven his talk is like the talk of those adults with whom he lives.

This may sound as though learning to use language is easy for the child, and indeed it is quite apparent that the young child has a tremendous facility for developing language, a capacity which seems to be an innate part of human nature. But it is not easy; the child persists from day to day making small advances, urged into this persistence by his need to be understood and his urge to communicate his wants and his thinking to others, and by the stimulation that others provide through their efforts to communicate with him.

In spite of the fact that all children come to speak and to use language, there is no doubt that they show very different skill in using language when they come to school. Teachers of young children are very much aware of these differences and of the effect that such differences have, both on the child's success in communicating with others, and on the responses he can make to the experiences provided for him in school.

If we listen to four year olds talking we will find some who demonstrate that they are already using complex patterns of language, as they produce long utterances which may show few irregularities or 'mistakes'. If we examine what they are saying we will see that they are able to use language for talking about events they remember, or for anticipating something that might (or might not) happen in the future. The child's stock of words, his vocabulary that is, may be large and he may express ideas with explicitness.

But all teachers know that this is not a picture of all children. There will be other children who at the age of four may talk readily, but whose speech may not be intelligible to others; others may not talk easily or readily, and so give the impression that their language resources are quite meagre. Other children may talk very readily, and we may feel that they are quite fluent, but when we consider what they are saying we find that much is repetitive, consisting of a commentary on the immediate present only and showing little complexity of thought.

Other children will be awkward in using speech, relying heavily on gesture, using mainly one-word answers and failing to be explicit unless urged by the adult.

Some children, clearly, do not fulfil the possibilities for using language because their parents are not aware of the experiences children need. Teachers, particularly those in nursery and infant schools, frequently meet mothers who come to them for advice or just to talk about their children, or to help in school. These teachers are in a particularly good position for drawing the attention of mothers to the importance of particular aspects of caring for children, especially during the years before they come to school. Much of the advice which can be given is of a commonsense kind, and some may feel that what can be said is so obvious that it is almost unnecessary to say it. In spite of this it might be of some value to look briefly at the stages through which language develops in the years before school, and at those experiences which seem likely to promote the development of language, and those which would seem likely to hinder it.

The stages of language development

Children learn to talk because we talk to them. We expect them to learn to talk, and from the very earliest days we talk to them as though they can understand something of what is being said to them. Even in the first weeks the baby begins to respond to the voice, by focussing his attention and listening, and by trying to bring his eyes into focus on the moving face in front of him. The voice must come to have some meaning for him as it becomes familiar and associated with the way in which he is handled, and with the routine activities of feeding, bathing and changing.

Soon the familiar voice comes to have a social meaning for him as part of the experience he has with other people as he responds to their attention. It is important to talk to the young child frequently, to give him the opportunities for responding to people's voices, and to help him begin to distinguish people from one another.

The social experience is necessary even for the very young child. He needs, of course, time for sleep and rest, but he should not be isolated from other people and their activities for long periods. If the child is left in his cot away from the rest of the family, or in his pram in a quiet corner of the garden where nothing ever happens, then he is being denied the stimulation of the general experiences of people and their voices and activities that life in the home

provides. The stimulation which the adult offers at this time is important, for the child is unable to seek experiences himself. Gradually the experiences of situations and sounds which occur together repeatedly become familiar, and this association provides some kind of meaning for the child.

By the fourth month the child is becoming able to play some part in the social exchange himself. He responds with smiles, thrusting his arms and legs in pleasure as people talk to him. He begins to discover his own voice as it emerges in coos and gurgles and cries, as he engages in the general movement of which his body is now capable. As his vocal sounds start and stop, so must he gradually become aware that the voice he hears is part of his own actions—and it belongs to him. Perhaps the most important experience at this stage is frequent attention from other people who talk to him and provide opportunity for him to have the kind of experience from which, it seems, he comes to control his sounds. This is done as the adult builds up a conversation-like exchange with him. He is gurgling away, perhaps, and mother or father turn to him and talk to him. Now the child listens and so his own voice is stilled. The adult stops, perhaps expecting the child to take his turn. If the adult is prepared to wait, the child will probably return to his babbling, and at another pause the adult may speak again. In effect the adult who acts like this is providing the child with an opportunity to learn about the social basis of talk, providing an experience which has the turn by turn character of conversation, and in which there is pleasure for both. Moreover, the experience is helping him to bring his voice under his control for gradually, it seems, he comes to recognize that the pause is intended for him, and he deliberately produces a sound in response to the other's approach.

We can see that by about five or six months old, the child becomes able to initiate an exchange quite deliberately as he calls out, or squeals and then waits for the response. We can see how important it is for the child to be amongst people for much of the time, so that he can become alert to their voices and their actions, and so that he can take pleasure in the social exchange which becomes the vital motivation for trying to distinguish the features of language at a later stage. But he cannot learn just because he is surrounded by voices. Without the social face-to-face exchange voices would remain unidentified. It is the relationships with people that are important. The child responds to people and in doing so he experiences the speech they use. Once this awareness and control of the voice, and the pleasure of 'conversation' has been established, it seems as though the child begins to use his voice less, at least for producing sounds randomly. Perhaps it is that his attention becomes engaged in the new experiences which increased mobility brings around the eighth and ninth months, when he begins to crawl and shuffle. Perhaps, too, his increasing control of his hands and fingers means that his attention is given to discovering something about the nature of objects and materials as he handles them, lifting them to his mouth and tasting them. The sounds he now makes are more deliberate and often provide an accompaniment to a repeated action, for example, as he bangs a spoon on the table or plate, and matches his voice to the rhythm.

At this period it is tempting to leave the child safe in his cot or his playpen with a variety of objects to explore for his own amusement. But we should not assume that because he is not able to imitate words he does not need to hear language being used. At this time the child begins to recognize that sounds often refer to objects and to people and their actions. He can learn, for example, that the sound 'ball' refers to the object that he plays with. If he hears the word associated with the ball frequently enough there will come a point at which he will demonstrate his understanding, perhaps by crawling away to find his ball which is in a cupboard, or hidden behind some piece of furniture. Even though he may not be able to say the word 'ball' we can recognize that the word when spoken by others has meaning for him. It is important then to talk with the child frequently, helping him to build associations between the sounds of words, and the objects or actions which they can come to represent. The meaning of 'No' begins to be recognized around the age of nine months, and can be seen to change the child's intention. It is probably a sound he hears frequently and becomes associated with inhibiting action. A little later we can see the child anticipating the curtailment of his actions and at about fifteen months old he may begin to say 'No' to himself, not, it is true, refraining from action, but rather anticipating the response of the adult.

But although the child at nine or ten months is not able to control his voice and imitate the sounds that others make, we can begin to help him to use the sounds he can make spontaneously, as words. For example, if he has a sound which has something in common with the word 'ball'—perhaps 'bow' or 'all' or even 'aw'—then the adult can help him to use this sound to represent the object. As the child uses the sound the ball can be offered to him as though he had asked for it. He is then likely at some point to indicate that the sound now represents the object, so he makes the sound as he reaches for the ball. The sound he makes will often move nearer to the sound the adult makes, and so the shaping of the word begins. This is probably the way in which most families help the young child to learn that sounds can represent objects and actions, that is they help him to learn what 'words' are for.

By twelve or fifteen months, the child who is helped in this way may have mastered between a dozen and twenty words based on sounds already within his repertoire. Before the child can enter further into language he must be able to imitate those sounds which are accepted as representations of the objects and actions with which they are associated, i.e. he must be able to produce recognizable words. As we have said earlier, the child can build up meaning for some words even before he can imitate them. Meaning is developed from his own actions and awareness of familiar experiences. Expectations are made clear to him by gesture and intonation as well as by the spoken 'word'. But as his ability to reproduce sounds in imitation of words and phrases increases, we can see that he acquires new possibilities for making his needs understood.

Although the ability to imitate sounds plays a tremendous part in the child's ability to acquire vocabulary and structure for his utterances, learning to use language is clearly much more complex than being able to imitate sounds. Imitation is not enough to explain how the child gains meaning and gains the adult's way of using language. The physical manipulation of objects leads the child to recognize the similarity between different objects and different situations. The demonstration of feelings and of attitudes imbues situations with important dimensions of meaning. The adult's priorities in using language to make clear one kind of meaning rather than another is also important. The whole environment, therefore, provides numerous influences which will affect the way in which the child will come to use language.

It can be seen from this that the talk in which the child is continuously engaged is most important for his development. The adult plays back to the child information that is needed for progressing a little each day. First in helping the child to gain single words which can be produced in sequence, in a form that is referred to as 'telegraphic', in which the embedding features of the adult form are not present. This activity begins to appear towards the end of the second year in most children, and remains characteristic of most children's talking until the second half of the third year.

Most adults seem to help the child quite intuitively as they talk, sometimes simplifying what they say to accommodate the child's immaturity, and sometimes speaking almost as they would to an adult or older child. Often they take what the child has said and repeat a corrected version, which sometimes the child will repeat himself immediately. In this way it seems the child gains the experience he needs for distinguishing the more ambiguous aspects of structure in talk, and gradually more and more of his talk gains the character of the adult's.

Late development of language

There are differences in the rate at which children develop language. Frequently parents worry about the child who is late in talking and wonder whether he is of low mentality. While this is not necessarily the case, it would be wise to advise them to look at the experiences and motivation they are providing to stimulate the child's learning. The child cannot learn if no one is interested in him, if he is left alone without stimulation, or if the meaning of the talk he hears is never at a level which is accessible to him. While he does not need simplified talk all the time,

he does seem to be helped by the use of simple structures some of the time.

Another cause of delay might be that the child is not strongly motivated to use language because everything he may be expected to communicate about is anticipated by the people around him. If this happens it is as though he were being deprived of the need to communicate. Children who have a rather easy-going disposition and who demand little attention may also meet too little stimulation and lack the motivation to communicate because they do little to demonstrate their need for attention themselves.

Many parents when they talk to teachers will express the view that their younger children seem to have learned to use language more quickly, and at an earlier age, than the first child. It is easy to see why this might be so. The first and only child has only his parents to talk with him, and is dependent on the time they can and are willing to spend with him for opportunities to hear and respond to talking. For the children who follow there will be the talk of the older child or children, who will not only talk to the youngest but also to each other and their parents. So for any child after the first there is probably more talk going on around him, even though he may not be involved in much of it. Once this younger child can control the sounds he makes, he learns many words and phrases by imitating his older brothers and sisters. But it is possible for us to be deceived about the learning that is taking place. The child may seem to talk a great deal, but the purposes for which he is learning to use language are likely only to be those which come readily to young children. Brothers and sisters who are not much older than himself are not likely to reason with him, or explain why or how things happen as they do. Nor are they likely to help him reflect on past experiences as perhaps his parents would. It is important, therefore, when talking with parents to point out that although being with other children may stimulate the child to talk more frequently, the child will not gain the variety of experience of using language that the interest and encouragement of the adult can give. It is important that parents make efforts to spend time talking with their younger children and do not feel that leaving them to the care of older children is the most beneficial experience for them.

The best advice that can be given to parents, then, is that every child needs their interest and attention and that this should start as soon as the child is born. Even the tiny baby needs the interest and stimulation of being with or near people, of seeing them and hearing their voices, and responding to their direct attention frequently as they care for him and talk to him.

As the child grows, the interest of the parents in his increasing ability in all directions, and in his capacity for responding to the world around him, is essential if he is to fulfil his potential. With this interest the parents are likely to talk with the child frequently, and it is through this interaction that the child's most important learning is accomplished. Through the use of language his curiosity about the world around him can be expressed and satisfied. Answering children's questions may become tedious, but the experience for the child is important, providing him with attitudes which will continue to support his need to find out and to know. The experience of using language that the child meets at home may be a crucial factor in determining his attitudes towards learning at later stages.

Chapter three

Language and learning in the home

It would be impossible to give an account of all that happens to a child or make an inventory of all that he experiences. The difficulties of making comparisons between the experiences of many children are therefore insurmountable. Nevertheless, it is possible through research to sample some aspects of children's experiences and to make comparisons of these. Even observations of parents and children together in different situations can allow glimpses of the kinds of differences in experience which might be of importance for the child's development. This is particularly the case when we consider differences in the experiences children have of using language in the home. Children can be observed daily in the streets with their parents, in buses and shops, in the launderette and the doctor's waiting room, and in or about the school with their mothers. The way in which language is being used in these situations can be revealing.

Although observations made in such situations may never reflect all that happens in the home, and certainly can never form a basis for testing any hypothesis, nevertheless they can help our thinking about particular problems. What happens outside the home may be in some ways different from what happens in the home because it is more open to the views of others, but it is likely to be based on the same values and practices which also apply in the home.

Such observations, therefore, can lead to some insight into the role that language can play in the child's development and the kind of opportunities for learning that seem to be offered to the child as the parent talks with him. Let us take two examples only to make some contrast. The following episodes are personal observations, but were noted down carefully as the incidents were happening.

Example 1

Nicky is just three years and two months. He is with his mother in the launderette. Mother is loading the drying machine with clothes. (Nicky N: Mother M: Manageress Ma.)

N: Let me put some in. I want to put them in.
M: Oh give up. Go sit down.
N: I want to—let me.
M: No—I told you no.
Nicky runs down the length of the launderette.
M: See, come back here. Come and put the pennies in, see.
Nicky comes back and mother gives him the coins to put in the machine.
N: It won't go in.
M: Here, I'll show you—like this.
Mother demonstrates.
N: Like this—in here—Oh.
The machine starts.
N: Why's it go round like that?
M: 'Cos it does. It's drying the clothes.
N: But why's it go round and round?
M: Oh, I don't know. Come and sit down now.
N: I'm going outside now.
M: No, you stay here—sit still.
Nicky complies—but then begins to crawl along the bench.
M: Come back Nicky—come and sit here.
Ma: Would he like a book to look at? There's a new one here someone's given us.
M: Oh he's no good with books—he just tears them. Come back Nicky.

Mother gives Nicky a slap and carries him back.

M: Now sit still and be good.

Ma: He might like to look at the funny man here.

N: He's a clown isn't it?

Ma: Yes, he is. Do you want to look at it?

N: Can I have it? Can I take it home?

M: No you can't—it's not yours.

Ma: Well, other children will want to look at it as well you know.

N: I'll have it now.

M: Then look at it quietly here. . . . Sit still and don't tear it.

Nicky turns the pages and looks at the pictures. He asks several times 'What's that?', 'What's it doing?' to which Mother gives one word answers, for example, 'A hoop', 'Jumping over'. After a few minutes Nicky abandons the book and returns to running about and crawling on the seat whilst Mother concentrates on trying to control him.

Example 2

A similar situation in which Peter, aged just three years, is with his mother. (Peter P: Mother M.)

M: Hold the door for me, will you Peter?

Peter holds the dryer door open.

P: Oo—it's warm.

M: Is it too hot for you to hold?

P: No (*he moves his fingers*) it's not too hot here on the edge.

M: Here we are then. Empty all the clothes in. (*She tips the clothes from the basket into the machine.*) Can you shut the door now?

P: That's a lot isn't it? Have we to put some money in now?

M: Yes, we need some fives. (*She looks in her purse.*) Here you are. Can you put them in? It will need two fives to dry them, I think.

P: I've put one in. It's going round fast now. I'm putting the other one in. Will it go faster now?

M: No—not faster, it'll go on spinning for longer.

P: How longer?

M: For a longer time, I mean, we'll have to wait longer for it to stop.

P: Why does it go round?

M: Well—you see—the clothes are tumbled about

and the water in the clothes runs out through the holes.

P: I can't see any holes.

M: Well—they're all covered by the clothes just now—but look up at the top when the clothes fall down—you can just see them. We can look at them better when it stops, though.

P: And does the water go out through the holes?

M: Well, some of it does, I think. But it gets very hot as well. You feel now—the door's hot, isn't it?

P: Burning, nearly. Does it make them dry?

M: Well, you know what happens when we put wet things round the fire.

P: Yeh, my coat went all steaming didn't it? When I went with my dad for some paint, didn't it?

M: Mm, you did get wet then. And that's how the clothes get dry—it gets hot inside and the water dries off. Now we'll have to wait. Can we sit down somewhere?

Peter runs off down the launderette. His mother sits down.

M: I think you're in the way down there—you'd better come and sit up here, I think. Can you move the basket out of the lady's way?

Peter stands watching the lady putting clothes into the washing machine, and then moves the basket to one side. He goes then to look at the comics and books. He stands looking at them before choosing one and taking it along to his mother.

It would, of course, serve our purpose much better if we could give longer extracts, or an assortment of extracts of the same mothers talking with their children. Even so, we could only use it to reflect on what the child might be learning if what was recorded here was typical of all the child's experiences. We cannot say that this is typical of either the mother's or the child's behaviour, but it is still useful to consider what the child would be learning if all his experiences of talk were of the kind we see here. It is true that Nicky's mother might give long explanations at home and that this kind of behaviour is used only when others are watching, or that Peter's mother only behaves like this because people are watching her and that back at home she would be much more like Nicky's mother in the above example. While it is just possible that this might be true of the mothers' behaviour, we would hardly make the same kind of suppositions about the children's behaviour. Peter is not likely to adopt an unfamiliar way of using language because others are watching; he is more likely to fall back on what he expects to do in similar situations at home.

Let us suppose then that these observations are typical of much of the experience that the two boys are having day by day at home. What would the differences be in the bases of their learning?

Both mothers are probably equally concerned about how their children behave, both at home and away from it, but the methods of ensuring acceptable behaviour are somewhat different. For Nicky, it seems there is a never-ending list of instructions when he is with his mother about what he must and must not do, and his attention is continually being directed to what is permitted and what is not. But these instructions do not seem to be either consistent or enforced and the general impression is one of conflict between the child's restlessness and energy, and the mother's need to have him complying with her wishes. There is little offered to him from which he can develop his understanding of why such behaviour is necessary.

Peter's mother does not seem to be so much concerned with enforcing a particular way of behaving, but the reader may feel that Peter responded very differently in this very similar situation. Was that just chance, or is that in itself likely to be an outcome of the kind of approach which his mother shows here?

Perhaps Peter's mother intuitively feels that the secret of an easily managed child is to engage him in the ongoing activity and to win his interest. Thus, if his attention is on the drying machine, and is held by talking with his mother about some aspect of it, then he is not so likely to make problems for control during this time. Perhaps, also, she is finding satisfaction in the way in which her child is able to talk with her in an adult-like way. She enjoys seeing him take an interest and beginning to understand. So the whole situation becomes a rewarding one for the child, one which he seeks to extend by asking questions and by offering new information. It is also, in some sense, rewarding to the mother. He asks questions about the working of the drying machine and why clothes dry, for example, and offers information from his own personal experience about getting wet when he was out with his father. So the child has become a willing partner in situations like this, where the mother, through her talk, encourages him to express his ideas to her.

But the difference between them is not that Peter asks questions and Nicky does not, it is rather that when they ask questions they tend to be met by very different responses from their mothers. Nicky's mother seems to turn his questions aside, claiming that she does not know the answer; Peter's mother tries to give some answer that will satisfy the child, even though she may not feel capable of giving a comprehensive and technically-sound explanation. This child's thinking is no doubt being carried forward, even by what might be to an adult an inadequate explanation.

So the kind of talking these two little boys are experiencing is directing their attention differently to the world around them, giving them a different view of it, as well as influencing the way in which they will come to use language with other people, reflect on their own behaviour, and consider other people's feelings.

To understand the extent of the differences in experience we would also need to look at many other aspects of life in the home: at the kind of play activities that mothers encourage, and the extent to which they enter into play with their children; the extent to which the child spends time in the neighbourhood with other young children, without contact with adults; the interest in stories and books that has been created by the parents; the extent to which visits and excursions become the basis for new exploration and new understanding.

Trying to get the measure of a child's experiences is difficult, but the important features will be the attitudes towards experience and values which he gains from talking with his parents. How much opportunity the child has for responding to others is clearly important, but the vast majority of children meet adequate experiences from which to learn to use language. Much more important seems to be the *quality* of what the child experiences, or the purposes for which language is used.

As we have already said, the examples can only help us to think about the kind of differences which might be occurring between children's home experiences. Most children experience a good deal of language which is aimed at controlling their behaviour in some way; perhaps the difference is more likely to be in the extent to which language is used for giving explanations and reflecting on the reasons for behaviour, as well as for examining interesting features of the world around, for imagining, and for thinking about other people's feelings. Children who experience talk used for these purposes seem likely to develop a different view of the world from those who rarely have such experiences, and naturally learn to use language themselves for these purposes.

But it may be, and the example of Peter and his mother might illustrate this, that using language in these ways reflects and induces ways of thinking which might be considered an essential part of the educated person's equipment. Those children who are helped to develop these ways of thinking and of using language bring with them to school the basis from which the kind of learning expected in school can spring: the essential tools for education are already being fashioned.

Children whose experiences are more like those in the first example may learn quite different attitudes and skills. Nicky's experiences of using language may be leading him in a different direction and to a different viewpoint. He may be learning that talking with the adult is not expected of him, that his questions are not answered in a way that brings any reward. Because he is not offered explanations, or expected to give explanations, he may learn not to reflect upon what he sees and hears, but to accept it at face value. He may learn to look to the adult for control, for permission, for physical comfort, but not to seek understanding of what happens around him. Children whose experiences have produced this kind of learning are likely to be at considerable disadvantage when they come to school.

What impressions of Nicky and Peter might the observer gain from conversations like those in the examples quoted above? It would be easy to explain the differences by saying that Peter is just more intelligent than Nicky. But it is important to remember that in the context of his own home Nicky's learned behaviour is as adaptive as Peter's; he has learned to cope with the world as it is for him just as Peter has. When they meet in school each draws on earlier learning to meet the requirements of the new situation; Peter's earlier learning generates responses which meet the expectations of teachers, while Nicky's earlier learning provides a positive hinderance to knowing what is required of him.

Much research now indicates that the child's early learning in using language will determine the way in which he is disposed to respond not only to questions and comments, but also to his experiences. In this country Professor Bernstein and his associates have investigated the differences in the responses which children from different social environments can make to the same experiences. The conclusions from such research are that children develop different systems of meaning as a result of their experiences of using language in the home. The world takes on a different character, according to the values and the perspectives which are developed towards experiences. Differences in experiences of using language will not only influence the way in which children respond to teachers in school, but will also influence the kind of responses they can make in intelligence tests. The experience that children have of using language in the home, then, may well affect the progress that the child will make in school, and it may also influence the kind of assessment that will be made of his ability.

The examples given here have been used only to illustrate how wide differences between children in their attitudes and skill in using language might be accounted for. We should note that many children may fail to meet the teacher's expectations when they come to school, not because they are lacking in potential but because their expectations of the adult are not in tune with the teacher's expectations, and also because they have learned to take quite a different view of their experiences from the one which is generally assumed in school. Their failure to use language to help them explore the many new activities offered to them is a reflection of their earlier experiences and learning.

We can see from this that many children will be at considerable disadvantage in school, partly because of what they have already learned about adults' expectations of them, and partly because of what they have not learned about ways of using language and the teacher's expectations. What should the teacher try to do to meet the needs of such children? We shall take up this question more fully in the second guide, *Talking and Learning*, but it creates something of a dilemma for the teacher. Should we try to change the way in which the child uses language? Will not such a change alienate him from his family? Is it not, in any case, attempting the impossible, when the child spends so much more time in his home than he does in school?

In the first place, what the teacher can offer to children might be seen as complementary to his experiences at home. We must be careful of the attitudes which we convey to the child; he must not be made to feel that he and his parents are rejected because of differences in speech which some would say were superficial differences in styles of speaking. But no one, surely, can deny any child the right to fulfil his potential for thinking about and understanding the world around him. Skills of thinking, and the ability to express ideas, are the rights of every child. The disadvantaged child particularly needs such skills, and the nursery and infant school may be the only place to offer him the necessary experiences from which they can be developed. The aim should be to help the child gain more from his experiences in school, and not to put him in a state of conflict with his home. But we might conceptualize the problem a little differently. Although what he learns in his home may not have given him the skills of communicating and thinking he needs in school, it may be that the consistent and continuing experiences that he has in his peer group are much more restricting than his home experiences. Many disadvantaged children spend much of their time in the company of other young children and are thus restricted to the kind of thinking and uses of language that such young children can stimulate for themselves. The problem for the teacher is to help the child to new attitudes towards language and learning in school, and to try to avoid reinforcing attitudes which have already developed that might prevent such changes being effected.

In these first three chapters we have tried to provide some indication of the theory that provides a framework against which we can set the practical work with children that the remainder of this book will be concerned with.

We have considered several questions. First, why be concerned with *language*? In chapter one we tried to show how language functions not only as a means of communicating and for conveying knowledge, and attitudes, but also how the very use of language promotes ways of thinking, examining and reflecting on experiences.

Secondly, we have looked at the potential that all normal children have for developing language and considered the experiences that parents need to provide for their children in order to promote the development of language.

Lastly, we have looked at the influence which experiences in the home have on young children. Particularly we have looked at contrasting ways in which parents might talk with children. We have tried to point out that although all children generally have experience enough from which to develop language, the way in which they will come to use it will depend on the kind of interaction which children have with parents. What children learn to do with language as a result of their experiences at home is likely to set up habitual ways of thinking and responding which will in turn affect the kind of response the child will be able to make to school experiences.

We go on from here to consider ways in which the teacher can set about observing and making judgments about a child's ability and inclination to use language.

How can the teacher discover what help each child needs if he is to profit from the experiences provided for him in the nursery and infant school? The purpose of this book is to explore a method by which the teacher can build a picture of a child's skills and problems in using language and to identify those who most need help.

Explorations

Learning to use language

Language and communication

1 Consider the teacher's comments below:

I've got a little boy in my class who doesn't say anything but he communicates very well without using any language.

Well, for instance, he goes and stands by the milk, just waiting, so I know he wants his milk. And when he doesn't want to do something he just sits and looks miserable, so I know what he's thinking. And he pulls at my skirt when he wants help. And he puts a lot into his pictures—I can tell what they're about.

Bearing in mind the points made on p. 8 on the definition of communication, to what extent do you consider the teacher's first statement is justified ? What evidence does she produce of communication going on ? What can we justifiably say is happening between teacher and child ?

2 Communication can take place without using language at all and often communication takes place with very little expressed in talk. Consider the following exchange:

Wife: Well ?
Husband: OK.
Wife: Did he ?
Husband: Yes.
Wife: Why ?
Husband: Well—you know what he's like—
Wife: Yes—that's it.

Suggest some situations in which this might have been a very meaningful exchange.

In what kind of situations can such limited use of language support communication ?

The development of language

3 'Up' and 'down' are often amongst the first words the child can respond to and then use. Can you suggest reasons why this should be so ? Consider the kind of experiences on which meaning would be based.

What can the mastering of the words 'up' and 'down' achieve for the child ? What does it enable him to do that he couldn't do before ?

What conditions are needed for the child to establish meaning for his first words ?

4 The following is an example of the child's early efforts to use words.

Jane, aged six, is playing in the bedroom with her two year old brother, Pat. Jane frequently points out colours to Pat and he has begun to produce the word 'pink'. On this occasion he stands by his cot, patting the sides and saying, 'Pink –mine pink'. Jane is delighted and echoes, 'Pink—it is pink. That's clever—very clever.'

A few minutes later, Pat turns to the bed and pats the pillow slips, saying, 'Pink, pink.' Again, Jane praises him, 'Good, that's right—it *is* pink.' She is very pleased and calls out to her mother, 'He said pink again and he's right!'

A few minutes later, Pat picks up the blue and

white hooped jug and shouts, 'Pink—pink!' Jane's face falls. We can see her expectations are shattered by this failure to recognize the colour and she exclaims, 'Oh no, Pat, it is *not* pink, it's blue!' Pat looks puzzled but murmurs, 'Blue' and strokes the jug.

Colour is a difficult attribute for the young child to recognize. Here, Jane is intuitively trying to help her brother to discover colour, without much success. In what way is the use of the word 'pink' helping Pat? A pink-striped pillow slip, a pink cot, a blue hooped jug—is there a common attribute? *What might Pat have learned from the above incident?*

Experiences of using language

5 Consider the following conversations between two mothers and their sons, both nearly four years old. We cannot know whether such conversations are typical of their predominant experiences of using language. We can, nevertheless, consider what learning the child would be gaining from such experiences.

Conversation 1

Peter is just four; he is travelling inter-city with his mother. He is standing on the seat, looking out of the window. His mother is reading a popular woman's magazine. (Peter P: Mother M.)

P: Look, mum (*he turns and taps her shoulder*)— cows!
(*Mother looks up, nods, and goes on reading.*)
P: Some water. What's that, Mum? What's it doing?
M: Come on, sit down, you'll make the seat dirty.
P: (kneels) It's going under a bridge now—what's it doing? That bird on the water?
M: It's a duck. Sit still—mind your feet.
P: It's got its head under the water—what's it doing?
M: Come on—take your feet down, sit down and keep still.
(*Peter sits down.*)
P: I want my cars—all of them.

(*Mother gets up and takes cars out of bag. Peter pushes them across the table.*)
P: They're going to London. *We're* going to London, aren't we?
M: Yes—be quiet now and play with your cars.
P: This one's like my grandad's, isn't it? It's got bumpers on.
M: Don't knock my bag down. Be still.
P: Look—an aeroplane! It's a big one. What's it doing?
M: I don't know—coming down.
P: Yes it is—coming down—zoom! (*He stands up again and presses against the window.*) How can it come down? Will it crash? How does it come down?
M: I don't know. Sit down and let me read, there's a good boy.

Conversation 2

John is not yet four. He is travelling with his mother and his baby brother, who is asleep. He is kneeling at the window and the train passes over a bridge, alongside a main road. (John J: Mother M.)

J: There's a lot of cars down there—look at them. What are they all doing?
M: It looks like a traffic jam, doesn't it? Or perhaps the traffic lights are stopping them—can you see?
J: There's a policeman and he's stopped them.
M: I wonder why he's done that?
J: I can't see what they're doing.
M: Perhaps there's an accident or something.
J: We're going fast now. Look, there's a river now—and some boats.
M: It's the canal, I think.
J: Isn't it a river? It looks like one.
M: Well, the river would be at the bottom of the hill, wouldn't it? Can you see, the canal is on the side of the hill?
J: Why is it there?
M: Well—because someone decided it would be a good thing to have it there, so that the boats could go through the town.
J: Do the boats go through the town now?
M: Some do, I think, but they used to bring all the coal from the mines in big boats.

J: Coal—for the fires?
M: Yes—like we burn on the fire.
J: Where do they get the coal?
M: Don't you remember? You saw men in the mine on the telly—do you remember?
J: And they had lamps on their heads so they could see.
M: Yes, that's right.

What do John and Peter seem likely to be learning from these incidents—about the world around them, about adults, about themselves, about using language?

If these conversations were typical of the experiences of these two children, what differences in their responses to school experiences might be expected?

Applications

6 Eavesdrop!

Listen to parents talking with their children, on buses, in shops, in the launderette, in the streets and schools. What are the children learning about people? about the world around them? about themselves? about using language? Note down some of these. In what way is the language experience influencing the child's interpretation of his general experience?

Get to know your tape recorder

7 If we want to study children's language, we can only do it through studying their talk and their responses to others talking. But somehow talking must be captured in order to examine it closely. A tape recorder is designed for this particular task.

There is a good deal of skill in using a tape recorder in such a way that it does not intrude upon what we are wanting to record. It should take a spool large enough to record for at least half an hour, and preferably an hour, without needing to change the spool over. This means that the machine can be switched on and off as it is needed, without drawing too much attention to the operation.

The most important thing is to have a good microphone which will not be too prominent, and one that can be placed in such a position that it neither restricts the child's activities, nor is likely to be knocked over. It is important also that it should not be placed on the table where children are working, otherwise the recording is likely to be distorted.

In practice, a longer and stouter lead than is generally supplied with a tape recorder is needed. This allows the tape recorder to be placed away from the scene of action so that it attracts little attention and the microphone can be suspended from a hook on the wall, or over the place where the recording is to be made, or clamped to a hat stand or specially-made stand, from which it can be suspended and moved from place to place on the floor and placed in such a position that it is not likely to be knocked against by children.

Teachers will need plenty of practice using a tape recorder, so that they are familiar with setting it up, switching it on and off, and with forward and backward winding. Practice of this kind should begin now, so that the teacher will feel confident about using the tape recorder in the classroom when this is suggested as an activity later on.

It would also be useful to set up the tape recorder in different situations, in the home corner, in a corner outside the classroom, and to record some talk. Listening to these recordings will indicate the kind of problems that are likely to be met, so that they can be planned for and avoided later.

Further reading

References have been made throughout the first chapter to the books that form the theoretical basis for this view of language. Teachers might like to follow up some of these references or, alternatively, turn their attention to less theoretical works, for a more practical view of the young child's language.

Chapters one and two of Joan Tough's *Focus on Meaning* give a very general impression of the characteristics of the young child's talk, and chapter four of Andrew Wilkinson's *The Foundations of Language* develops these ideas. Another review of this aspect of language is to be found in chapter one of M. M. Lewis's *Language and the Child*.

LEWIS, M. M. (1969) *Language and the Child* NFER

TOUGH, J. (1974) *Focus on Meaning* Allen and Unwin

WILKINSON, A. (1971) *The Foundations of Language* Oxford University Press

PART TWO

The social use of talk and
problems in using speech

Chapter four

The concept of appraisal: a plan for action

When children come to school we know that they have already learned a good deal about using language. By the age of three most children are using language readily, and we ought to be very concerned if a normal child comes to school at the age of five without well-developed skills in using language. But we have already made the point that children's experiences of language being used in the home are very different, and therefore what they have learned to do with language themselves is also likely to be different. Some of these differences will have an important effect on the child's ability to respond to the experiences we offer to him in school. It is therefore important that the teacher should be able to recognize both the skills and the problems the child has in using language, so that he can be given the most effective help.

How can the teacher become aware of the kind of skill each child has in using language and recognize any particular difficulties he has in communicating with other people?

If we were considering children's physical development we would expect there to be considerable differences between children in their physical growth and physical skills. How could such differences be discovered? Some could be quickly and indisputably established. Measurements could be made of some physical attributes such as weight, height and girth. It would also be possible to give the child a number of tests. We could see how high he could jump, how far he could stride, how heavy a load he could pick up. When we had the results of all the measurements and tests, however, the picture would still not be complete, and some of the most important information that we needed might not be readily accommodated by measurements or tests,

but might only be assessed by close observation. How does the child walk and run? What is the quality of his movement? What kind of control does the child have of fine and intricate manipulation and of movement that needs concentration of strength and effort? What is the child's general coordination of movements like? Is he awkward and ungainly or does he move easily and smoothly without apparent effort? Many of these qualities would defy measurement, and many would defy comparison with other children. But all could be appraised i.e. described in terms which build up a picture of what the child is like. Such a picture could not be described as an evaluation of the child's physical skills since it would not compare him with any particular standards or norms. But it could perhaps be described as an *appraisal*, a picture of what the child was like, a picture of what he could do and his manner of doing it. This is the sense in which we use the term *appraisal*. The most appropriate approach for the teacher to take, in order to discover what needs to be known about each child's development, seems to be through making appraisals and not by tests and measurements.

There are some measurements that could be applied to the child's language. We could count the number of words he used in each utterance and find the mean; we could count the frequency of the use of different kinds of words—nouns, verbs and pronouns. We could also count the number of utterances showing different kinds of complexity, for example the use of clauses. All these could be regarded as measures of different aspects of the child's language; but they would tell us little about the purposes for which the child was using language.

Generally, tests are used in order to set the child's

ability to use language against a standard which has been derived from the responses of many children to the same test. Thus we can discover how he compares with children of the same age.

Just as measurements and tests cannot tell us all that there is to know about the child's physical ability, neither can they tell all we need to know about the child's ability to use language. Tests cannot tell us when, or for what purpose, the child will use language, nor how he is disposed to use language to add to his stock of knowledge, and understand the world around him. Tests cannot tell us how the child will use language in his dealings with other people, and may only tell us something about the child's ability to use language in test situations.

Most measurements and tests are designed to examine the child's mastery of the language system. For example, they can tell us whether a child knows how to indicate plurality by adding 's' to nouns, and whether he has learned the exceptions to the rules (for example that we say 'mice' and not 'mouses'), whether he can make verbs agree in person and number, and add 'ed' for past tenses, and whether he knows that there are some exceptions (for example that we say 'went' and not 'goed'). Tests can tell us something about the knowledge that the child has acquired about the language system, but they tell us little that cannot be discovered by listening to the child for a few minutes and talking with him. Tests can tell us something about the extent of the child's vocabulary, but not about the way in which he will use it.

Tests and measurements, then, seem to tell us even less that is important about language than they can tell us about physical development and skill: they certainly cannot tell us the most important things we need to know about the child's use of language.

Measurements of the kind described above are inappropriate for other reasons. They require representative samples of the child's talk to be recorded and then transcribed and closely analyzed. While it is useful to do this in order to learn about children's use of language, as we shall recommend later, it is not something that can be done for every child in the class on the scale that would be necessary for objective measurement.

There are other quite practical reasons why we would not recommend the teacher to rely on tests. For the young child tests seem to be inappropriate because we cannot assume that he understands their purpose or that he will be ready to cooperate. We cannot rely on getting a picture of the child's ability to use language—only of his ability to respond to tests. Tests are also seen as unsuitable because they take the teacher away from classroom activities, and so take time away from working with children and promoting development. To avoid this, testing may be undertaken by someone who is less well known to the child, to whom the child is less likely to respond, and in these circumstances a representative picture is not likely to be gained. This is not to say that tests are not useful for some purposes. Diagnostic tests, in which ample time can be spent with each child, are useful in the hands of specialists, but they take more time than the teacher can usually manage.

It is because testing and measuring young children's language seem neither desirable nor practical, nor likely to provide the full picture of the child that is needed, that this guide to appraisal has been developed as a more useful alternative. From careful, informed observing it seems likely that the teacher will be able to recognize any difficulty the child has in using language, or the absence of particular uses of language which seem to be important. If problems can be recognized as the teacher talks with the child, it ought to be possible to offer help at that point, or to design situations to meet the child's needs.

The advantages of making an appraisal through observations are several. It allows the child to continue his normal activities. Making an appraisal does not take the teacher away from the classroom, or interrupt or curtail talking that arises spontaneously. It permits the teacher to select those situations in which the child is ready to talk so that talking provides both an enjoyable social experience and an opportunity to observe the child's spontaneous use of language. Most important, perhaps, is that where a natural talking situation is used, there is the possibility that some new learning by the child will take place at the same time.

Observing in this way also allows the teacher to

discover the extent to which what is said to the child is influencing the way in which the child responds. It allows different approaches to be made and the teacher is able to observe whether the adult's language is setting problems for the child.

In principle, it would seem that any situation in which the child is talking is one in which some appraisal can be made. Particular situations have been suggested in this guide in order to illustrate a method of working which depends upon listening to, and talking with the child, but the method can be extended to any situation in which listening and talking can go on. The suggestions are made so that they might serve as a starting point from which ways of working in other situations can be developed. The needs and interests of particular teachers of particular children, or even the conditions in particular classrooms, may lead to different modifications and developments.

We have used the word *appraisal* then, quite deliberately and see it as quite different from the concepts of *measurement* and *evaluation*. We are not advocating that teachers should try to place the child in any category, or rank him against other children. *Appraisal* in our view means building up a picture of a particular child, being able to recognize what he is already able to do in using language and discovering what he may not yet be able to do by talking with him. *Appraisal* means keeping the child's growing skill in using language in view, as a guide to the action that the teacher might take. *Appraisal* means that the skills of observing, of reflecting on what is observed and of using language with the child to promote his learning, are being drawn on continuously. In this way we can see that each time the teacher talks with the child it becomes an opportunity both for appraising and for fostering the child's use of language.

Since the skills of *appraisal* will always provide the basis from which *fostering skills* will be selected, our task must first be to examine the skills of appraisal which the teacher will need to acquire. The purpose of this book and the accompanying suggestions for practical activities in the classroom is to help the teacher establish the skills for making an *appraisal* of children's skills in using language. *Talking and Learning*, the book which is to follow, will then be devoted to the additional skills that teachers need in order to foster the development and use of language in young children through the normal activities we provide for them in school.

Approaching the task of appraisal

The teacher's view of a child is often influenced by what is already known about the child's background, and perhaps by experiences of dealing with older children from the same family. The teacher may already have certain expectations about the child which will influence the view taken of him. Impressions of each child are also built up from the talk and activity of the classroom, and from the kind of situation in which talk with the child arises. Some children are clearly quicker than others to respond; some are easily distracted whereas others persist; some are disruptive and others get on easily with everybody. Without some systematic method of checking impressions the teacher may gain a distorted view of the child. It is possible, for example, that because a child approaches the teacher frequently, or because he has a loud voice and his talk is heard above other children, the teacher will form a picture of a friendly, talkative child, or perhaps of an aggressively dominating child, whereas at some times and in some situations, he may not talk easily, and be quiet and submissive.

But the reverse might also happen. A child who never comes along to talk to the teacher, or whose voice is never heard above the rest, may be judged to be unfriendly or very shy, or morose. Yet the child who talks readily with the teacher may not be so ready to talk to other children. The child who never approaches the teacher might chatter happily to his playfellows. The child who never seems to talk in the classroom might talk easily with his brothers and sisters in the playground. The child who appears to talk readily with anyone may do so only to satisfy his immediate wants and may use little talk to extend his imaginative play. The apparently aggressive, disruptive child may sometimes be quiet and withdrawn, attracting little attention to himself.

If it is difficult to gain an accurate picture of a child's general personality and behaviour from chance encounters, it is even more difficult to form an accurate view of his ability in using language. The quiet child may have considerable skill in using language but be unable to demonstrate this when the teacher is near. The voluble child may be repetitive, his talk full of inanities.

If then an appraisal of the child's ability to use language is to be a sound representation of his actual skill it can only be achieved by planned and accurate observation.

But first we must decide what there is about the child's use of language that can be observed, and therefore appraised. What is it that teachers need to know about the child's use of language and how can that knowledge be gained?

Before going further we will define the terms we will use in referring to the several different aspects of language.

We shall use the term *language* to refer to the system of signs which is used to convey meaning. We can readily recognize that *words*, which make up what is generally referred to as *vocabulary*, are labels that have an agreed use. Words have a commonly-held core of meaning for those who use the same language system, otherwise communication would be impossible. There are also elements of meaning attached to words which are unique to the individual, or shared by a group which follows a particular interest or way of life.

The way in which words are ordered also offers a means of conveying information, for example the inversion of the order of words is used to indicate a question. There are also a number of devices for modifying the meaning of words, for example, the added 'ed' to indicate that whatever is being referred to lies in the past. Other devices indicate the link between words, for example 's' is added to the verb to indicate the third person singular. Such aspects are referred to as the syntax of the language, and the rules that govern the ordering of words and making agreements are referred to as the rules of syntax and the various formulae for linking words are referred to as syntactic structures. They are all part of the grammar of the language, and all have a part to play in expressing meaning.

When we talk about the child's use of language, then, we are referring to the way in which the child draws upon this accumulated knowledge of the language system, knowledge that is held intuitively, not with awareness, to convey some meaning to those who talk with him. We can only gather evidence of the young child's ability to use language from what he says, and from the way in which he responds to what other people say. When he is older, there will also be evidence from what he writes and from his response to the written word as he reads and as he grows older he will also be able to think about language and comment on aspects of the use of language.

But since we are concerned in this book with the language of young children, we must essentially be concerned with studying the child's use of language by observing his *talk*, and his responses to the *talk* of others. Frequently the terms *talk* and *speech* are used as though they were synonymous, but we shall distinguish between the two. We shall use the term *speech* when we are referring to aspects of the production of speech, that is to the activities of articulating and ordering sounds to produce words, and the term *speech structures* when we are referring to the application of the syntactical rules which govern the ordering of words and making agreements between words as we use speech. We shall then reserve the term *talk* for referring to the meanings which are conveyed, that is, the purpose for which speech is being used.

We will consider three aspects of the child's use of language that play a part in communication, and that should be observed if an appraisal of the child's ability to use language is to be made:

1 the *social use of talk*
2 the *production of speech*, including the *maturity of speech structures*
3 the *purposes of talk*.

1 The social use of talk

Language is developed because of the need to communicate with others. It can only arise in social situations. Meanings have to be shared and words and structures must be used consistently if language is to be a means of communication. The first thing to be discovered about the child is the extent to which he relies on talking for making and maintaining relationships with other people. We generally take into account the way in which children talk to others as we make judgments about their social adjustment. We refer then to this aspect of the child's use of language as the *social use of talk*. Perhaps it is the first view that we should try to gain of the child when he comes to school and a view that we should hold in mind throughout his early years in school. Unless the child is able to talk and express his meaning, his intentions and his needs, it is difficult for the teacher to form a view of his capabilities in using language and to give him the help he needs.

2 The child's production of speech and maturity of speech structures

We have already pointed out that we shall use the term *speech* to refer to the child's articulation and ordering of sounds that form words, and *speech structures* to refer to the application of the rules of ordering words and making agreements between words in speech.

The child may have problems in using speech which are not so much problems of using language but simply problems of producing speech; these may prevent communication taking place since they hinder other people understanding what he is saying. It is important then to discover any problems the child may have in using speech so that he may be helped to overcome such obstacles to communication.

3 The purposes of the child's talk

We shall use the term *talk* to cover the way in which the child uses language, i.e. the purposes and the content of what he communicates. In this sense we are referring to the child's meanings, his thinking and the kind of information he is using language to convey.

The three aspects of the child's talk that we have outlined above are each important in the act of communicating and they offer a logical sequence for progression towards the skill of making appraisals. In considering the task of appraising children's use of language we shall need to examine each aspect, and observe the child in some way in order to discover his problems and his needs.

In completing part two we shall consider the child's disposition to talk to others in order to discover any problems he has in making relationships with others. We shall then go on to observe whether he is at all frustrated in his attempts to communicate, by problems in producing speech, or by immaturity in speech structures.

In part three we shall consider the observations that can be made of the purposes for which the child is disposed to talk and suggest a range of situations which together should present opportunities for discovering the kind of help the child needs if his skills of communicating are to be progressively extended.

In this way, the reader who follows the suggestions for practical work with children, and who persistently reflects on and analyses what has been observed should, step by step, establish the skills that are needed for making the appraisal of children's use of language an integral part of classroom practice.

Chapter five

The social use of talk

The sampling approach

How shall we begin our study of children's social use of language? First of all when children start school, or when the teacher meets a new class, it is important to gain a general view as quickly as possible of each child's readiness to use language in school. The extent to which, and the way in which, the child talks to other people is an indication of his adjustment to life in the classroom, and of his relationships with other people.

Trying to gain a general view of the child's readiness to use language is something that can be planned and carried out systematically. With so many children to care for the teacher cannot watch every child closely all day, but a method which depends on regular sampling of the child's activities during one half day has been found to help the teacher to identify those children who most need encouragement in using talk and in making a better adjustment to life in the nursery or infant classroom.

Many experienced teachers who tried out the recommended methods were sceptical at first about the value of the sampling checks we suggest. Although they felt that the method offered something to new teachers, they felt that the experienced teacher was intuitively aware of children who had problems or difficulties. They found, however, that it was possible to misjudge some children considerably. Some children whom the teacher had judged not to be talking at all were found, on closer observation, to have a rather quiet voice and manner, but to be talking readily with other children and to have much greater skill in using language than the teacher had thought. Some children, who were thought to be getting on well because they

talked readily with the teacher, were found on closer study not to be talking very readily with other children. There were many surprises, and many experienced teachers were convinced that the regular sampling observation ought to be built into every teacher's practice.

These *sampling* observations depend upon the teacher keeping in mind one or two children during one half-day session. In this way, in the space of a week or two, a check can be made of all the children in the class, and those who need special help can be identified. At regular intervals the teacher looks for the child and notes what he is doing, perhaps as talking with another child or group of children ends, or some routine task is completed. If the child is settled at some occupation which absorbs all his attention there may be little to observe from a distance, although it will be useful to note the child's demeanour at that point. There is a great deal of difference between the child who is absorbed in some individual activity and is pursuing it with interest and determination and the child who sits alone, looking unhappy and gazing apprehensively round the classroom. There is a difference again between the child who sits alone, shrinking from other people, and one who sits with eyes full of interest watching the activity of other children even though he is not joining in.

If at the time of observation the child is pursuing an individual activity, the teacher should jot this down, together with some note about the child's general awareness of others around.

If, however, at the time of sampling, the child is talking and playing with other children then the teacher might observe from a distance for a few minutes, noting down the children to whom the observed child talks, and the kind of relationship which seems to be present, the extent to which talk is being used and gesture seems to be relied upon for communication.

If children are at a distance when they are observed there is still a good deal to be learned. What they are saying may not be heard but the expression on a child's face, the gestures he makes and the responses he evokes from others can be observed. If the child talks to other children, initiates conversations, or approaches adults, for example, this would be important to note. It would also be important to note whether the child ignored other children or listened to them but did not participate in the ongoing talk. Attitudes to others can be judged from the child's demeanour, when he is alone or with others, for example, shyness, friendliness, aggression, dominance, fearfulness of others, should be noted.

Some situations seem to be particularly profitable for observing the child's readiness to talk because communication of some kind—talk or gesture—is usually likely to take place, for example:

1   as the child arrives in the classroom
2   as he takes leave of his mother
3   as someone comes to collect the child
4   as he leaves the teacher and his friends
5   as he seeks help with his activity
6   when in dispute with other children
7   as he seeks help for his personal needs
8   as he seeks permission for some course of action
9   as he approaches the teacher to initiate conversation
10 as he responds to an adult in any situation
11 as he plays with other children.

If observations can be continued throughout the morning or afternoon for a few minutes at a time, this might produce five or six samples of the child's behaviour, and this may or may not confirm the impression that the teacher has already gained of him. Such observations should not wholly occupy the teacher. It should be possible to observe *and* carry on the general work of the classroom because a *sampling* procedure means close observation for only two or three minutes at a time. The teacher

will not be following the child round, making a note of everything he does, but will be deliberately looking up from other commitments from time to time to see what the child is doing at that point, and then making a note. Observing for two or three minutes, on perhaps five or six occasions during the half day, builds up a picture of the child, his relationships with others, his readiness to talk, and the variety of experiences he is meeting.

From a practical point of view, it is as well to start the session observing two children. Often it is possible to make sampling checks on two children during a half day. At each pause to observe, the teacher will look across the room for one child, make a note, and then centre attention on the other child for a minute or two and make a note.

Sometimes a child may be out of the teacher's view for a while, in which case observations can continue of the other child, and a note might be made when the other child reappears.

The purpose of such sampling observations is to note the extent to which the child is talking in the classroom. At this point it is not intended that the child's talk should be recorded or analyzed. The purpose is to find a method of discovering those children who for some reason are *not* talking, or who are not talking much in the classroom, so that they might be more closely observed and the kind of help they need can be decided upon and put into effect.

For many children the sample check will reveal that they are using language readily, that they talk with adults and children, that they can approach the teacher, and that they generally are using talk as a means of getting along with other people. For these children there will be no need for further checks, unless for some reason the teacher becomes worried by a change of behaviour, for example a usually pleasant child may suddenly appear ill tempered and aggressive, or a lively child may become lethargic and dreamy. Such changes should alert the teacher to the need for further observation to discover whether the child is having other problems in or outside school.

Where the sampling checks show that children are not using talk easily, or not talking at all, then the teacher will need to consider a plan of action for encouraging the child to talk more. We shall discuss ways of helping such children in the next chapter.

Keeping a record of observations

If it is important to build up considerable knowledge about the child and the extent to which he uses language, then it seems essential to devise some way of keeping a record. It is obviously difficult to remember all the details of every child's progress, but if notes are made regularly then it is possible to build up a picture of each child and the problems he seems to have in approaching and responding to others. These records would not be kept for any length of time, although they might provide useful information to be incorporated in the profile of a child's general development; they are seen mainly as an aid for making judgments about the child's progress in using language for getting on with other people.

The choice of a method for making records will depend on personal preferences and the priorities in any particular class. Some teachers may prefer to keep anecdotal records of children's progress which include comments on interesting features of a child's behaviour. Such records have the advantage of allowing the behaviour observed to be described in its context. The information collected in this way would provide the detail for a full, diary-type record.

Others may prefer a schedule for recording observations, and this will have the advantage of presenting a clear picture in tabulated form. It may not, however, contain the detail that can be recorded in a diary-type record.

Devising a way of making notes about a child's behaviour that takes little time, and causes little distraction, is not easy and requires careful thought. It is important to work out a method that the teacher will find appropriate and easy to complete and summarise, but it *is* important to find a method of making a written record, otherwise time spent in observing may not be fully effective because some points may be forgotten.

We can only suggest that teachers should go on experimenting until a method is found that suits

them as individuals in their own particular situation, and which allows them to follow the child's progress in adjusting to and making relationships through talk with other people. A method of recording is needed that will show the different situations in which the child is disposed to talk, or not to talk, and the extent to which the child can respond to other children and adults, and approach other children and adults in school.

Some suggestions for recording

We include examples of three methods of recording which have been found to be useful by many teachers.

Method 1

This is a diary-type entry and needs the least preparation since all that is required is a blank sheet on a tear-off notepad. The child's name is written across the top, together with the date on which the observations are being made (see page 40).

Each time the teacher is able to observe the child from a distance, or talk to the child for a minute or two, the time is noted, and important points are written down. Is the child alone? If not, who is he with? A note should be made of the names of other children or adults concerned, and also of the child's attitudes to others. For example, is the child friendly, aggressive or fearful? Does the child talk at all? To whom? Can anything be heard of what he says? If so, a note should be made of some of the actual comments used. Does the child approach other people? Does he respond when others approach him?

In the diary-type method, the teacher has little reminder of the points which should be noted. It may be useful therefore to have at hand a list of the points to look for, as given on page 43, so that it can be referred to during the first attempts, and discarded as soon as reminders are no longer needed.

At the end of the half-day session there should be five or six entries representing perhaps between ten and twenty minutes of observation, and by using the notes and reflecting upon the observations when the children are no longer there, the teacher can make a short summary of what seemed to be the important characteristics of the child's behaviour and disposition towards others. The page from the note pad can then be included in a personal folder kept for each child (together with examples of drawings and writing once the child begins to write) or in a folder in which notes on all children in the class are kept, clipped together for each child when more than one recording has been made.

Method 1

Johnnie Smith   12th October 1975

9.05	Brought mother into classroom to see hamster. Shouted 'Can I give him some apple Miss H?' Ran after mother—waved. Joined Peter S in sand—demanded sieve—some talk.
9.30	With Peter and Brian at slide. Shouting 'Watch me what I can do.' Each trying to outdo the other—friendly rivalry.
9.50	Sitting alone drinking milk; shows interest in blocks construction beside him. Pushes blocks over—shouts 'Sorry' as Bill threatens him.
10.30	Absorbed in painting picture and has difficulty controlling brush. Speaks to Miss H first. Replies 'It's my dad and that's his car.'
11.15	On outer edge of group listening to story. Restless, rolls on floor, Miss H speaks to him, looks abashed and sucks his thumb.
11.40	Sees mother, leaves group, speaks to Miss H. 'Want my painting.' Runs to show it to mother.

Summary
Johnnie is rapidly adjusting to others. Quite confident with other children and teacher.
Approaches and responds. Excitable and easily distracted. Needs help in listening with group.
Must make a point of looking at books and telling story to him alone when possible.

Method 2

This is similar to Method 1 but gives the teacher some reminder of the points to be noted. Columns are used to organize comments on the kind of activity at which the child is seen, the character of his talk and behaviour each time he is observed, and the actual comments heard.

This method of recording needs more preparation than Method 1, and a sheet or a pad would need to be quickly ruled out and headed for each child observed. If this method is found to be the most useful, then sheets could be duplicated and the amount of preparation would be no more than for Method 1. The information would be organized in columns so that summarizing would be done more easily.

Method 2

Tom Reynolds   14th October 1975

Time	Activity	Character of talk and behaviour	Utterances heard
9.10	Mother pushes Tom into classroom— he stands alone, looking after her. I offer my hand and welcome him.	No speech: takes hand: comes to sand tray	none
9.30	Still in sand: digging with hands, lets sand run through fingers.	Seems to be listening to Brian J and Jimmie C.	none
10.10	Washing his hands slowly. No response when I speak to him.	Withdrawn—seems timid—watches other children.	none
11.00	Sitting in rocker alone. Miss B asks Brian J to rock with him.	Lowers head: looks apprehensively at Brian but rocks with him.	none
11.45	Stands looking out of window.	Tell him mother's coming soon: sucks his thumb.	none

Summary
Tom was not seen to speak to anyone during the observations. Mother reports that he talks a lot at home. Some evidence that he is beginning to accept Brian J. Perhaps it would help if mother stayed longer. Will invite her to stay and help Tom to try out other activities.

Method 3

Many teachers have found this method takes the least time during actual observations, although more time must be spent on preparing the form. Any advantages that the method has are only realized if the form is duplicated and can be picked up and used immediately. This form lists aspects of the child's behaviour under three headings: participation in classroom activities, talk with other children, talk with adults. A number of columns is provided which should be enough to cover the opportunities the teacher is likely to have for observing during the half day.

When the teacher pauses to observe the child the time of observation is filled in at the top of a column and the observed behaviour is ticked. There is also a place for making comments on general behaviour and for summarizing what has been observed during the session. In analyzing the observations it is possible to see at a glance, by looking across the columns, the kind of behaviour which frequently occurred or did not occur at all, and any outstanding characteristics should be noted—for example that the child was never seen to talk at all, or that the child only spoke to one child, or only to adults.

Although some may feel that important information is not included here, the method should provide a profile of the way in which the child is using talk. Those teachers who find this method useful could modify it so that more information is included if this can be done without making the form too unwieldy.

Method 3

Child's name: Wendy Brown Date: 30th November 1975						
Time of observation	9.30	10.05	10.35	11.00	11.15	12.10
Participation in classroom activity						
Child alone and not involved in any activity						
Child alone but watching others						
Child absorbed in some activity alone	√					
Child following own activity but aware of others						
Child participating in a group		√		√	√	√
Talk with others						
No talk observed						
Child playing and talking to self, not aware of others						
Child listening to others but not talking						
Child talking and aware of others but not requiring responses from them						
Child initiating conversation and seeking responses		√		√		
Child directing behaviour of others		√				√
Child being directed by another						
Talk with adults						
Initiates conversation with teacher			√			
Responds when approached by teacher				√		
Maintains a dialogue easily				√		
Maintains a dialogue with difficulty						
Contributes when with teacher (in a group)				√		

General behaviour characteristics
Any particular features of behaviour that emerge
(e.g. friendly, confident, aggressive, dominant, shy,
shows lack of concentration).

friendly, confident

Summary of observed behaviour
Wendy appeared very confident and moved around the classroom easily, engaged in a variety of activities and completed each before moving on. She involved other children in conversation and responded eagerly with a lot of talk when the teacher approached her.

Selecting a method of recording

Some teachers might not feel that any of the three methods shown here is the most suitable for them; these examples are provided only as starting points from which teachers might work out a method which they feel is more suitable. Some teachers suggested that a checklist of behaviour which might be observed could be used, but in practice many teachers found that a checklist was unwieldy. Having a list to read through before making observations, particularly at the first attempt, served as a reminder for those using some form of diary-type, or running commentary record. Below is a checklist which teachers might like to refer to during first attempts at recording observations.

A reminder of points to note when observing

1 Note child's name.
2 Note time of observation.
3 Note type of activity child is engaged in e.g. home play, blocks, sand, water, clay, painting, looking at books, puzzles, construction materials, imaginative play, physical play, clearing up, taking milk.
4 Note whether child is alone or with other children or adult.
5 Note the extent of child's talk, e.g. single words only, short comments, talking readily, asking questions.
6 Note nature of child's approach or response e.g. friendly, timid, aggressive, abusive, demanding, rejecting, instructing, complaining, co-operating, apologetic.

Making a summary of observations

It is important to make a summary of what has been observed at the several points during the half day. This needs to be done as soon as possible after the observations have been completed since the teacher will need to reflect on all that has been observed, and look back to remember anything that may not have been noted down. The summary should point out any persistent characteristics of the child's behaviour, for example that he was never seen to speak to anyone, or that he rejected all approaches whether from child or adult, or that the child spoke readily to other children but did not speak when the adult approached him. Or contrasts in behaviour might be pointed out, for example that the child rejected other children's approaches when he was busy with puzzles, but joined in readily with talk in house play.

Each of the records given as examples tells us something about the child's behaviour that might not have been noticed had he not been observed. It will naturally mean more to the person who made the observations because for that person the notes and short summary made at the time are a reminder of a whole episode, which the record helps to recall.

For some children—those that appear friendly and who appear to be involving themselves through activity and talk in the life of the classroom—there will be no need to make further observations of this kind. But if the observations reveal behaviour very different from what was expected, then further observations are called for in order to discover what the actuality is. It is possible that for some reason a child may behave quite untypically on the day chosen for observing him. Here are some questions that might be asked about the child's behaviour in order to consider the overall picture of his behaviour.

1 *Observation of those children selected as apparently well-adjusted and talking readily*
    Was the child ready to talk in all situations or did he talk only to adults or only to children?
    Did the child sometimes settle down and pursue an activity on his own?
    Did the child seem to be leading other children through talk?
    Was this the case sometimes, or often, or always?
    Did the child appear generally friendly to others or was he frequently or occasionally aggressive?
    Was there anything surprising or new about the behaviour of an apparently well-adjusted child who seemed to talk readily?

2 *Observation of apparently quiet children*
    Was the quiet child really not talking?

Did the quiet child talk to anyone at all? If so was it to another child, brother or sister, or to an adult?

Did the child talk readily to children but seem to avoid the teacher?

Did the quiet child take part in any activity? Which?

Was anything surprising or new discovered about the quiet child?

3   *Observation of less-settled child*

Did the child appear unsettled when observed throughout a morning? Did he ever appear settled? In what situation?

Did the child move from activity to activity?

Did the child have a good relationship with anyone? If so, was it with a child, a teacher, or some other adult?

Did the child play alone mostly or did he join in with others at all? In what situations?

Was anything surprising or new discovered about the child?

The value of observations

Observations of this kind are likely to provide information from which it will be possible to assess what is likely to help each child most, and in one group of children, even where age is about the same, there are likely to be quite wide differences in their needs. For example, the following five children were all in one nursery group. These are the general pictures which the teacher had built up after they had been in school for a few weeks.

Michael rarely speaks in the nursery, and when he does so is almost unintelligible. He is a nervous boy; his speech is slurred and he makes himself understood mainly by gestures. Although he appears to listen, it is very difficult to know whether he is understanding what is said. Sometimes it is obvious that he responds correctly to instructions given to a group, not by understanding the instructions, but by copying the behaviour of other children.

Paul talks a lot but he is very difficult to under-

stand, although on the whole other children seem to know what he is saying. He is very persistent, and does not appear to be upset if he has to repeat something several times because the adult does not understand him.

Christopher would always prefer to listen rather than talk. He gets his sister to ask for things for him rather than approach an adult himself. It is very difficult to know what language he can use for he speaks so rarely, and he is certainly not using language to find out about the world around him.

Mark usually speaks quite clearly when he is talking to an adult, but when he is excited the words come in the wrong order, or he becomes frustrated because he cannot get over to people what he means.

Karen much prefers to talk to adults, and will listen to them without interrupting. With children she is quite the opposite, interrupting and taking over the conversation. She is very domineering, taking the lead in play situations and the adult role in the Wendy House. Other children do what she says.

Considering the needs of these five children, it seems fairly clear that a boy like Michael will need much encouragement to talk, to make good relationships with other children and to establish confidence in using the various activities provided. Another session of general observations in a few weeks time should inform the teacher of his progress.

Paul, on the other hand, seems very well adjusted but is frustrated by not being able to speak so that others can understand him. In the case of this child a short period of close listening might identify the particular problems of articulation that he has, and help might then be given or sought for him. Chapter seven will suggest ways of making this kind of observation.

Christopher's problems at this point seems to be the most extreme. He really needs a great deal of help if he is to become confident enough to talk in school. Some discussion with his mother might indicate if it is a problem associated with coming to school, and in this case encouragement and support should help him to make a better adjustment to life in school. However, if it appears from what she says that this is a more deep-seated problem, she might be advised to seek professional advice.

Mark and Karen are using much language but it is clear that they need help if they are to make better relationships with others. It would seem appropriate now to make a closer observation of the skills they have already developed in using language.

Before concluding this section, it is perhaps useful to summarise the points that have been made in this chapter:

1 Sampling of the child's behaviour over one half-day is not enough for judgments to be made, but against a background of other knowledge of the child such sampling can indicate to the teacher the way in which the child is developing. If the observations surprise the teacher in any way, a further view would be needed to check the impression: for example, if the child was normally an active talker but had been seen to be quiet and unresponsive on this occasion, sampling within a few days would be needed again.

2 Sampling observations of this kind might advise the teacher about whether a very quiet or a very aggressive child was gradually making progress or was regressing. In the case of such children, frequent sampling of this kind would lead the teacher to decide whether professional help was needed.

3 Where sampling confirmed that a child was making good adjustment and seemed to be using language readily, the teacher might feel that when the opportunity arose she could try to get a closer view of the child's ability to use language. She would also feel that perhaps general sampling of this kind is needed very infrequently as a check. Judgments of the child's behaviour would be influenced by the length of time the child had been in school.

4 We would not expect a child relatively new to school to display the same competence in making use of a variety of activities, or getting along with others, as one who has had much longer in which to adjust to school. Similar behaviour from a new child and a child who had been in school longer, would be judged differently.

5 The child's choice of activity might be a reflection of his disposition, and the view of the child's behaviour might be influenced by the situation in which he was observed. For example, group activities such as construction play, the home corner, water play, provide good opportunities and need for getting along with others, in contrast to more individual activities such as doing jigsaw puzzles, looking at books or drawing, in which the child might wish to be on his own. We might judge the child to be quiet because he is absorbed in an individual activity. Sampling can tell us whether he always chooses individual activities or whether he also chooses to be with others at some time.

6 If, from a sampling of this kind, one of the following views had been gained, it should be seen as a matter of some concern:

   a child was seen to speak to no one or to speak only to the adult during the half day
   a child was always domineering, aggressive or abusive towards others
   a child was seen to avoid the adult
   a child was seen to talk a great deal but was not involved at all in the ongoing activities.

Observations as a guide to action

Finally, we would like to emphasize that making the kind of observations that we have outlined here is only the first step towards making an appraisal of the child's use of language. Observations of this kind are needed in the first place to discover how all children are relating to one another and to the teacher and other adults. For many children the first observation will show that they are talking easily and readily with children and adults alike and the next step will be to take a closer look at the purposes for which they use language, that is, at the kind of information which is contained in their talk.

The first observations of other children may show

that they talk readily to children but not to adults. In this case the teacher and other helpers will need to make special efforts to talk frequently in an easy friendly way with these children, in order to win their confidence and encourage their ready approach to adults.

Other children may be found to be at ease in talking with adults and unable to talk easily with other children. They may be aggressive and threatening to other children, or they may be fearful and timid. In this case the teacher and other helpers will need to make special efforts to help these children get on better with their playmates. There need, however, be no delay in making a closer appraisal of their ability to use language if relationships with the teacher are good.

Other children may be found through the observations to talk to no one and to be quiet and withdrawn. The special help that needs to be given to such children is discussed in the next chapter.

Other children might be found to have problems in making themselves understood because they have difficulties in producing speech. We shall discuss such cases in chapter seven.

For those children who are seen, as a result of observation, to have problems of some kind in talking with other people in school, the teacher will need first to take action to help them to overcome these problems. It will then be necessary to make sampling checks, of the kind described, after a period of two or three weeks, in order to see how the child is progressing, and such checks may be needed for a considerable period until they indicate that the child is talking easily with others. Once it is seen that children are at ease talking with others, the next step in making appraisals is to work more closely with the child in order to discover the purposes for which he is using language. We shall consider in detail how the teacher can set about making appraisals of this kind in chapter eight.

Explorations

The social use of talk

1 How well do you know your children?

Comment 1   Sandra

I know all the children in my class—if I didn't I wouldn't consider that I was a very good teacher.

This statement was made by an experienced infant teacher before carrying out sampling checks on a number of children in her class. After checks had been made the same teacher commented:

I wouldn't have believed how wrong I was about Sandra. She is always coming to talk to me and she talks easily with me. I had thought she talked to everybody else, but when I checked I found that, although she always seemed to be near other children, she never talked to them, even when they spoke to her. I must try to help her join in and play more with other children.

Comment 2   Barney

A nursery teacher commented, before carrying out observations on Barney:

Barney never talks in school. I don't know whether he has not developed language or whether he just doesn't want to talk. He never talks to me or to the nursery assistants. I don't think he says one word to anyone all morning!

After making the sampling check on Barney, this teacher made the following summary:

I was completely mistaken about Barney. Each time I located him he was involved in some activity with another child and he was saying something to someone, or someone was speaking to him. He didn't seem to get excited or shout, or gesture much, so that you wouldn't notice he was talking unless you were watching him closely. When I sat down in the book corner with him he responded quite well but he has such a small voice it's not easy to hear him unless you are very close to him. His voice would never attract attention and I wonder now if he doesn't try to talk to me because he's learnt that people have difficulty in hearing him.

I talked to his mother for the first time. She says Barney talks a lot at home. But she has a very quiet manner and a low, soft voice. It must be very peaceful in their house!

Comment 3   Sheila

A third teacher commented about her class:

I haven't any quiet ones, I wish I had, all my children talk all the time.

Amongst those children on whom she ran a sampling check was Sheila, and these were her comments after observation:

Sheila's not very big for her age and I think I must have overlooked her before. She gave an answer when I spoke to her, just a short one, but I couldn't tell what she said. I never saw her speak to anyone else and much of the time she was on her own, playing with jigsaws or pegboard. In fact, she never moved from that table until play-time. I think she needs help in trying out other things and in approaching other children and I must try to find out what her speech difficulties are.

Considering these examples, is it possible that there are children in your classroom that you really don't know? Could you be misjudging some children? Consider some of the conditions and practices which operate in nursery and infant classrooms which prevent us knowing our children well.

For what reasons is it important that children should be using talk easily with children and adults in school?

What would you expect to discover through listening to children talking?

2 Discovering more about children

How can teachers discover more about children in their classes? Consider the sampling methods of observing children described in the previous chapter. What can the teacher do to make such checks possible?

The following report came from a group of teachers:

We didn't know how we would manage to carry out sampling checks at first, but we all managed it quite well and now we are using the method all the time with new children and with those we have found who are having difficulties in making relationships. We try now to keep these children in mind and talk to them and try to draw them into playing or working with other children. Every now and then we do a sampling check to see how they are progressing in their attitudes and interaction with others.

These are some of the things that paid off:

1   Have a jotter and pencil in your pocket all the time. When you've got a minute to look and see what the child is doing you can make a note on the spot, quickly.

2   Those who had some other adult in the class-room found they could observe one or two children every morning and afternoon, and after the new class had had time to settle in and get to know children and teachers, they found they could discover which children were having difficulties over a spread of two weeks.

3   Sometimes we discovered in the first hour of sampling that the child was talking readily to children, teachers and helpers and had no difficulty in using speech or in getting along with others. The sampling check was not needed again for these children and we then began to look for opportunities to look more closely at how they used language.

4   The sampling check helped us to identify those children who had problems of communication, or of making relationships, and we concentrated on helping them first.

5   So even if there isn't permanent help in the classroom, where there is an extra teacher in school, or other assistant on the staff, it helps if they can spend more time with each class so that there is someone to help when the teacher is trying to make the sampling checks.

6   Teachers in nurseries generally had no problems in observing. Infant teachers found it more difficult. Sometimes the headteacher helped, some people had one or two mothers in the class-room who could relieve the teacher at least of routine tasks and could keep an eye on children's activities.

7   Where no help was available at all, the organization of classroom activities was very important and teachers found that they needed to plan activities at least for parts of the day, when children were busily engaged in play and other activities which did not need the teacher's direct supervision all the time.

5   Some teachers with older children found that observing at playtime and dinner time, and when children were in the cloakroom and going home, showed the kind of relationships children were setting up.

What kind of problems do you anticipate in your classroom when you try to carry out sampling checks? Do the above reports suggest to you ways in which the task might be made easier—or just possible? What preparations can the teacher make so that observing for short periods at frequent intervals can be undertaken?

3 What can be recorded?

Many teachers have found that it is helpful to have some plan or form for making a note about observations. They have also found that a brief summary at the end of each recording can help to build a continuing record of the child's progress.

The following methods have been tried. Consider whether any seems likely to help you.

Method 1   Diary-type jottings

Judith: 4 years 5 months   7.11.1975

9.30   J making crayon patterns. Chooses carefully. Speaks frequently to Ian F. Talks about pictures—comparing efforts.

9.55   Picture dominoes with PH (nursery assistant). Names pictures—asks questions—shows interest—selects cards appropriately.

10.20   Sitting at table with IF drinking milk. Friendly—smiles—'Is your milk cold? Mine is.' Spills—fetches cloth and mops up competently. Says to PH 'I spilt it—sorry!'

10.50   In house corner with IF—'I'm making tea—do you want some?' Pretends to put water into teapot. Pretends to pour tea for IF. Offers it—'Here you are.' Busy laying table—puts pan on cooker—'What do you want for dinner, IF?' Barbara B approaches—'Go away, I'm, playing with Ian!' J accepts BB staying and involves BB in making dinner.

11.30   Still in house corner. Now alone, singing and talking to herself and dolls. Others pass by. J unaware, engrossed in putting dolls to bed.

11.45   With PH for story. Sees mother—runs, waving picture—'I did it for you!' Mother smiles—bends down to look—happy reunion.

Summary
J seems well adjusted, has made friendship with IF. Can assert herself but quickly accepts others. Good relationship with PH. Talks readily, concentrates and becomes involved in activities.

Method 2   Diary-type 2

Darren: 4 years 4 months   21.11.1975

	Activity	Observation of talk and behaviour	Utterances
9.15	Comes in with mother. Runs to seesaw—sits on and pushes—no one to play with him. Runs back to mother. Kisses her, waves and goes back to seesaw.	Quick, controlled, confident. Affectionate towards mother—mother interested—watches him.	Watch me! Did you see me? Give me a kiss.
9.50	Playing with bounce-back equipment. Runs easily. Good control of ball. Competent overarm throw.	Leader of small group. Takes the initiative. Catches ball—gives it to others—can take turn. Continuous comment—friendly towards group.	That was a good shot. I throwed it on the net. Now Peter—my turn. Have another turn. Throw with one hand. He catched it. Come on, Barry—it went through my legs.
10.15	Busy with large blocks. Places blocks carefully. Looks for blocks of suitable size.	Cooperating with other children. Offering advice and directions. Leads imaginative play.	It's an ambulance. We're making an ambulance. It's coming to the town. It's a fire engine. Ding dong! There's a fire in that house over there. I'm a fireman. I've got a fireman's hat at home and a badge.
10.25	Having milk, eats orange and biscuits. Takes empty cup away. Tidies table.	Alert—sensible, competent. Obviously enjoys lunch. Responds to NA.	I'll get my own milk. It's nice, this. I've put it away.
10.50	Painting—mixes paint— holds brush easily. Uses large strokes. Picture of house— controlled.	Concentrates—not distracted by children passing. Thoughtful.	That's my house. I'm painting it red. I'm going to put my bike there.

Summary
Darren is physically well controlled, alert, eager to join in, friendly towards other children. Tends to lead. Good attitude towards adults, wants to help. Talks easily to anyone. Enjoys imaginative play.

Method 3 Check-list type

	9.30	9.50	10.10	11.15	11.30	12.15
Child's name: Lee Martin 4 years 8 months	*Date:* 5.6.75					
Time of observation						
Participation in classroom activity						
Child not involved in any activity					√	
Child watching others in a group						
Child in some activity alone		√				
Child participating in a group						
Child following own activity but aware of others	√		√			
Talk with others						
Child playing silently		√				√
Child playing and talking to self, not aware of others						
Child talking and aware of others but not requiring responses from them			√			
Child initiating conversation and seeking responses	√					
Child directing behaviour of others						
Child being directed by another						
Talk with adults						
Initiates conversation with teacher				√		√
Responds when approached by teacher	√ (vaguely)					
Maintains a dialogue easily						
Maintains a dialogue with difficulty				√		√
Contributes when with teacher (in a group)						

General behaviour characteristics
Any particular features of behaviour that emerge
(e.g. aggression, dominance, shyness, lack of concentration)   Shy, lacks concentration when in a group. Dreamy.

Summary of observed behaviour
When Lee speaks to an adult his conversation consists of one sentence or two words only. When asked a question he replies, 'What?' or 'Don't know'.

Look at the three methods of recording. What seem to be the strengths of each type of recording? What kind of information about a child's use of language would be useful to have as a part of a permanent record?

Applications

It would be useful now to try out the methods of observing represented here to discover which method of recording you find most valuable. Make sampling checks on children in school and record your observations using the methods suggested. Consider the form of recording and try to construct one which seems most suitable.

Consider the evidence of your sampling checks. Do they confirm your previous views of children, or is there something new to add to or change your view?

Further reading

Questions of this kind are discussed in chapter six of *Focus on Meaning*. The topics discussed include the situations in which children can be observed, and the problems that some children have in talking to others, and in producing speech.

TOUGH, J. (1974) *Focus on Meaning* Allen and Unwin

Chapter six

The child who does not talk

Identifying children who do not talk

Of all the problems that the teacher meets, perhaps the child who does not talk in school should cause most concern. It is difficult to understand the nature of the child's problems, since he is unable to tell anyone just how he feels, and why he cannot talk and respond to others. The teacher may expect children who are just starting school, or who have changed classes and are amongst children they do not know, to be rather quiet and shy for a few days, perhaps even for a few weeks. It is understandable, too, that if the teacher is unknown to the children it may take a little while before they can approach her easily. But after the first few days most children are likely to be confident enough to approach other children and the teacher, even if they are rather hesitant. If the child is still not talking to anyone after the first few weeks in school the teacher should rightly be worried and should consider the special help that the child might need.

There are several possible causes for a child not talking readily, and it is important to distinguish between these. It is also important to distinguish other characteristics of the child's behaviour, for these are likely to indicate the intensity of the problems of which noncommunication is just one symptom.

The teacher is likely to become aware in the first few days of meeting new children that some are less ready to talk than others, but unless she spends time in observing the child, the impressions that are gained may be misleading.

The sampling check which we have recommended as a means of discovering how children are using talk in school should help the teacher to identify children who are unable to talk at all with others. As we have already pointed out, the sampling check will perhaps lead to the revision of the teacher's view of some children. Amongst these may be children who were thought not to be talking to others.

Some children, who perhaps were thought not to be talking because they never approached the teacher, may be shown by the check to be talking quite readily with other children, but not with other adults. Others may be found to respond to the teacher and other adults when spoken to, but perhaps are rather quiet in temperament, and have quiet voices which means that they accept too readily a situation in which they can not easily gain attention in competition with other children.

In some cases, then, the teacher will discover through the sampling check that although some children do not find it easy to approach others, or assert themselves, they are using talk; but they will need encouragement and the opportunity to build up relationships and to become bolder in their dealings with others. It will, however, be clear that they are using language and can talk with others when conditions are not too overwhelming for them.

Where the sampling check confirms the teacher's impressions that a child is rarely using language, or never talking or responding to other people, then closer observation will be needed. At the same time, the teacher should try to fill out the picture of the child by talking with his mother and other teachers or adults who know him, in order to try to discover how severe the child's problems are. The teacher will want to discover whether the child talks normally at home and outside school, and the explanations of his difficulties that the child's mother might offer. Perhaps it is just the problem of starting school—there may be some aspects of school which alarm the child. If so the teacher should be able to take steps to change any threatening situations and to spend time supporting the child in school until he is able to relax and make relationships with children and other adults. But if the child has problems in using talk at home or outside school, or his problems continue in school, the teacher should discover from the mother what she thinks might have caused the child's problems and begin to build up a picture which will help in identifying possible causes and also in deciding what steps should be taken immediately and in the long term.

Before we consider the kind of observations we should make of the quiet child, we will examine briefly some conditions that might give rise to a child's inability to talk to others.

Some causes of the child's inability to talk

Physical causes

We know that there are certain physical conditions which make it difficult for the child to develop language. We would expect such conditions to have been diagnosed long before the child comes to school, because the lack of development of language is due to abnormalities from which mental retardation results. We shall not discuss problems of this kind here. It is possible, however, for the child to have a degree of deafness which has not been recognized before he comes to school, which will make it very difficult for him to distinguish speech clearly in the talk of those around him and therefore he will have great difficulty in developing language normally. But in this case noncommunication would be only one symptom of his problem. The child would not be responding normally to other sounds in the classroom: for example, he would not be startled by shouts, or by activity that was going on beyond his view, or even respond to his name unless directly approached. The teacher who suspects that the cause of the child's problems is deafness should not hesitate to discuss it with the headteacher and the parents and arrange for the necessary tests to be made.

Children of deaf parents may also have some problems in developing language since they may not have normal experiences of hearing language. Usually, however, this is a problem of which doctors and health visitors are very much aware, and arrangements are likely to have been made for the child to be in contact with normally-speaking adults.

Neglect and deprivation

Sometimes the child who does not talk is considered by the teacher not to have developed any language. It is difficult to judge how many children above the age of three, by which time language is normally well established, do not talk because they have not developed any language. Even if the child is retarded he is likely to make efforts to talk. The child who does not talk at all is not the same as a child whose talk is immature, babyish, or telegraphic, as is the talk of most two year olds.

Children learn to talk by being stimulated to talk by others, and if that stimulation is missing in the first three years then the child may not have the necessary experiences from which to develop language.

Problems of this kind have been associated with children who have been brought up from their earliest days in institutions, where there are many children of the same age and few adults to provide continuing relationships and stimulation. Even in such conditions, however, the development of language is likely to be retarded and not absent altogether. There are, perhaps, few institutions of this kind nowadays.

In what kind of conditions could children *not* meet adequate experiences of talk? Where children are badly neglected, left on their own, or with other young children, for long periods, they may also not meet adequate stimulation. In such cases it is not only the development of language that will be affected, but there are likely to be other signs of retardation.

Some children in large families may be mainly looked after by brothers and sisters who are little older than themselves, and so may not be stimulated enough by adults, but we should be very careful not to imply that all young children in large families will not meet adequate experiences of language.

Where parents and older members of the family take great interest in the younger children they may be particularly well stimulated and benefit accordingly.

Problems of this kind may also result from children being left for the major part of the day with childminders, who may not only fail to provide stimulation for the child to talk but may also actively inhibit the child from talking by insisting on quiet, acquiescent, passive behaviour and who may punish and restrict what would be considered to be normal development in talking, playing and exploring.

Some children, then, may not talk because they have not yet had enough experience of talk from which to develop language. If this is the suspected cause then there are likely to be other signs of neglect and perhaps ill-treatment. The child may be fearful, dull and unresponsive, trying to avoid attention and showing an inability to play or move about; he may look lost, dejected or confused. Such a child has problems which are more extensive than problems of communication and the teacher will need to draw the headteacher's attention to him and find what help is available for checking how serious his situation is so that something can be done to curtail such neglectful and damaging treatment. These are the children who may have been deprived of many normal experiences, not only of using language but also of care and affection. Treatment in school must take the form first of reassuring the child and winning his confidence, and then providing frequent stimulation: playing and talking with the child, and wherever possible giving him the experiences of using language that the normal home would provide, for without this he can make little progress.

For the most part, however, where a child is abused and illtreated, language will accompany whatever is done to him, and is likely to be one of the means by which rejection is conveyed to him. Fear and depression may make such children unable to talk in school, but most will find school an environment in which they are accepted, and will look to teachers and other adults for the attention they lack at home.

In those families, however, where there is a criss-cross of talk from several adults and other children, and perhaps a confusion of sounds from radio and television, the young child may find it very difficult to distinguish talk addressed to him. If in such conditions no one finds it necessary or important to talk with him, but expects talk to arise from the child himself, then the child may have difficulties in establishing language. His problems may be accepted by parents who think that the child is slow to learn, and that little can be done to help him. If once he can walk the child then spends much of his waking time with other small children in the street, we can see that he may come to school without a normal development of language. Where the teacher suspects that this may be the case, then it is important not only to provide the child with many opportunites for learning to use language from talk with the teacher and other adults in school, but also to discuss with the mother and father how he might be given better experiences of talk at home.

Emotional causes

Often the causes of children not talking in school are those that stem from emotional problems of some kind, and are due not to an absence of appropriate stimulation to use language or to physical conditions, but to problems of relationships with other people in the family. The range of problems is so wide that we cannot discuss them fully here, but they would all seem to result from the child feeling rejected, unwanted, or failing in the sight of those he most wants to accept him.

Problems can be caused by thoughtlessness on the part of parents, who do not appreciate that young children are interpreting what they see and hear but cannot be objective or reason about their experiences. For example, being constantly and unfavourably compared with other older members of the family, or even with more precocious younger members, may make the child feel he is always fighting a losing battle to keep up with his parents' expectations. Being ridiculed, teased and generally made miserable by overstrict demands, may also make the child retreat. But very different conditions may also make a child unable to face life outside the home, for example when a child is made to feel that he cannot do anything for himself, but must always rely on his parents for making decisions. Such dependence may develop in a kindly, indulgent, overprotective home, or in a punitive, restrictive home, and one of the results may be that the child is not able to make relationships easily with others.

Perhaps the most acute problems arise when some sudden happening changes the kind of relationships the child has come to expect. The new baby arrives and suddenly distracts everybody's attention and may make the child feel alone and unwanted: he may become naughty and spiteful in an effort to gain attention, or he may retreat into himself and in turn reject those who have caused his feelings of not being wanted.

The child can also feel that he is deserted and unwanted whenever he is separated from those he knows well. This is particularly true during the early years when he cannot understand that the arrangement is only temporary. Perhaps his mother disappears from his life because she is ill in hospital, or must go away for other reasons. Even though he may be well cared for by others, the familiar routine, the ways in which he is handled, are upset and replaced by the unfamiliar; he feels lost and may again become awkward and complaining, or reject both those who tend him and those who have caused him such unhappiness.

If the child must go to hospital, he may be too young to understand the reasons and any pain he has there may be associated with his unhappiness at being away from home. Shock at separation, then, can cause problems, and permanent separation— for example when a parent dies, or the child is abandoned, or one parent leaves home—can have a long-lasting effect.

There are other conditions at home that may set up problems. Parents may be so concerned with their own difficult relationship that the child is neglected or caught in the middle and may feel threatened and insecure. Such conditions may lead the child either to disruptive behaviour, almost as a protest at what is happening to him, or to withdrawal, a condition in which it seems he prevents himself from responding to the unpleasant happenings around him.

It is difficult to understand why a child should react by not talking to anyone, but it can be seen to be a way of avoiding further hurt and rejection. The problem is that this retreat brings him no help. Often people will feel that it is best to leave him to get over his problems on his own, and then the condition may become more established as a way of behaving and more difficult to change.

The child may respond to disturbing situations in other ways, for example by daydreaming, by fantasy, or by adopting imaginary companions who somehow compensate for or dispel his feelings of rejection and insecurity.

Understanding why a child responds by refusing or being unable to talk is not easy, and it is frustrating for those who try to help him. It seems likely that the child's own temperament is a factor in determining the way in which he will react to traumatic conditions. Some children, for example, may be severely affected just by being lost for some time, while others will remain apparently unscathed by such an experience. The kind of response a child can make may be dependent on his earlier experiences and such an event is likely to be more damaging to the child who is already insecure.

However, whatever the causes, if a child is severely withdrawn, not making contact with anyone after some time in school, then the teacher must regard this as a case which needs urgent attention. It is not enough to hope that the child will grow out of the condition.

Observing the child who does not talk

In order to distinguish the severity of the quiet child's problems, close observation will be necessary, and observations should be made in as many different situations as possible. A diary-type record will probably be most useful, but a list of important aspects of behaviour to be looked for and noted might help the teacher at first. The following list of points might be copied down and kept at hand while making observations:

1 Note in what situation and to whom the child speaks: Note also how he speaks e.g. mutters, turns away, looks embarrassed or confused, and

for how long he maintains contact using and responding to speech.

2 If the child does not respond to others by talk, note whether he responds in any visible way e.g. by the expression on his face, or physical action. Note whether he is pleased, tolerates or rejects the approach, through gesture or action.

3 Note in how many situations in which the child is approached there is no evidence that he is *aware* of the approach i.e. he does not hesitate in his activity, or there is no change in facial expression. Note which people arouse some awareness, some recognition, even if only a fleeting glance or change of expression.

4 Note whether the child ever plays alongside other children. If he does, note whether he pauses to watch them, or remains apparently unaware of them.

5 Note how the child responds if others push him, or threaten him. Does he appear perturbed or is he quite unmoved?

6 When the child is alone note if he is:
> busy and absorbed in some activity
> pursuing an activity but aware of, and watching, others
> passively inactive: sitting, standing, or lying down on his own but not visibly distressed
> apprehensive and shrinking from possible contact as others pass him
> moving away from others as they approach as though deliberately avoiding them
> engaged in compensatory self comforting, for example, thumb sucking, rocking, masturbating
> engaged in compulsive aggression for example, banging his head, twisting and pulling his hair.

7 Note any other evidence of insecurity, for example, changing behaviour with mother or older brother or sister, temper tantrums, persistent crying, persistently pursuing an activity that he perhaps regards as 'safe'.

The pattern of behaviour that emerges from such observations should give some indication of the severity of the child's problems. If he is responding at all to others, or showing some interest in what is going on around him, then he should respond to encouragement and the teacher's approaches, and with support begin to accept children's approaches.

If the child is passive and unresponsive, seemingly unaware of children even when they bump him, and makes no visible response to anybody's approach, then there is cause for alarm.

Information to be gained from others

In order to fill out the picture of the child, the teacher should discover what other teachers may know about the child and his family, and discuss the child's behaviour with his mother. It is important to discover how the child behaves at home and what conditions may be responsible for his behaviour.

Answers to the following questions should be sought:

1 Does the child not talk at home, or with playmates, or neighbours or to other people when he is out with his parents?

2 If the child does not talk in any of these situations, has it always been so? If not, when did such behaviour appear? Did anything happen about that time which might have upset the child?

3 Has the child been threatened by what might happen to him at school if he is naughty? Has he been told, for example, *not* to talk or play in school, and that the teacher will punish him if he does?

4 How do the parents regard the child? Are they setting too high standards for him? Is he being compared with other children in the family? Is he rejected as a nuisance, or as a baby by brothers and sisters? Do the parents think the child is just slow? Have they tried to help the child to talk or do they think that children should not be encouraged to talk? Are they overprotective, overindulgent, restricting, or punishing?

5 What kind of relationships does the child have with his mother? With his father? With brothers and sisters?

6 Is there any reason to think that either parent is mentally depressed?

7 Is there any evidence that there is violence in the

home directed at the child, or other children, or the mother or father?

8 Is there unhappiness or conflict in the home, illness or any other condition that could lead to the child feeling rejected and insecure?

From close observations of the child in school, from observation of him with his mother and brothers, sisters and playmates, and from discussion with teachers who know the family, and with the child's mother and father, the teacher should begin to appreciate the extent of the child's problems and the possible causes. From this total picture she will begin to see what possible action she might take to help the child.

Helping the child in school

The reason why a child is not talking in school may stem from a number of different causes and his condition may be more or less severe. Discovering what seems likely to be the cause may guide the teacher in taking what steps she can to reduce the child's problems outside school. In school, however, the approach must be to show concern for the child, encourage play or activities with any child or adult that the child seems able to accept, and carefully build up a relationship between the child and the teacher which will help him to take part in the activities provided in the classroom. Leaving the child on his own for long periods in the hope that he will in time begin to approach others seems likely to make it more and more difficult for the child to change his established pattern of behaviour.

The child needs reassurance and a relaxed atmosphere. He needs constantly to see that people care about him, without feeling that pressure is being put on him to do what does not come easily to him. How can the teacher show interest and understanding and also offer a permanent invitation to the child to join in any activity?

The teacher will need to be sensitive to the kind of contact that each child can accept and be ready to draw back if the child seems in any way disturbed by the approaches.

Sometimes the child will respond to the teacher's outstretched hand and the invitation to see what other children are doing. The teacher could make a tour of the classroom, stopping in the usual way to talk to children in turn, helping and encouraging their efforts, and including the quiet child in her comments from time to time, directing his attention to anything of interest.

If the child is not able to accept accompanying the teacher in this way, then it is important to try to place the child near to other children playing but sufficiently protected from any robust activity and to leave near to him interesting materials—books, table toys, jigsaw puzzles, crayons and paper— which he might take up and use himself. A smile and a comment from the teacher from time to time, and the activities of other children near him, may in time help the child to begin to join in.

If the child seems apprehensive of other children and is not ready to accompany the teacher, then from time to time the teacher should make an opportunity to sit down beside the child, perhaps working at something which might interest the child, making a model in clay, doing a jigsaw puzzle or looking at a book. The teacher can comment on the activity to the child, even though he makes little response.

In every way possible the teacher should demonstrate interest in the child and concern for his well being. Any effort the child makes should be supported quietly, perhaps only with a nod and a smile. The teacher must be very careful never to overwhelm the child by her comments, or by drawing the close attention of others to the child, or by making him an object of fun or ridicule.

The child who is naturally rather quiet is likely to begin to join in activities with other children, perhaps after some initial hesitation. He is likely to continue to be rather quiet in all his dealings with other people.

The shy child may need support and encouragement until friends are made, but gradually shyness should wear off and the child should begin to join in activities, gaining confidence and making relationships with others more readily.

The child who is withdrawn and unresponsive after some time in school is the one that the teacher must be most concerned about. The teacher should try to establish a relationship with the child, and demonstrate care and concern for his well being, encouraging any efforts to respond.

If little progress is made during the first weeks then, after discussion with the mother, expert help should be sought. In the meantime the teacher should remain tolerant and continue to demonstrate care and interest and hold out to the child frequent opportunities for responding to talk and activity.

Explorations

The quiet child

Identifying problems

1 The quiet child in the classroom should always cause concern to the teacher, although it is easy to overlook such children since they cause her no disruption or overt problem. The following observations were made by Miss Smith, a young teacher of a reception class. The school admitted children at the beginning of the term in which they became five years old and the first observations were made after the children concerned had been in school two weeks.

A number of questions should be borne in mind while reading the observations.

Is the behaviour shown during the session seen to some extent in many children of this age or is it so unusual or extreme that it gives cause for concern?

What can be learnt about these children from the observations and how much more in each case would the teacher need to learn of the child and his background before deciding on a course of action?

Does the reader see evidence of change in the reports of Martin's and Jean's behaviour and if so, what does this seem to indicate?

Child study 1 *Martin: 4 years 8 months*

Newly arrived in area. Nothing known of family except particulars given to the headteacher on entry. Mother living on her own—no father. Martin showed no emotion on entering school and his continuing withdrawal is causing concern. Time has been allowed for settling in and the usual attempts at drawing him into activities have been made, but with no apparent success.

Observation 1 16.9.74

9.05 Martin, as usual, impassive as mother took off his coat. She talked to him but he did not respond. I went over to talk to both of them. M turned head away. Suggested she come to school at 3.20 for a chat about M, while Martin in other class for story. Mother settles Martin at bricks and then leaves. Martin does not look up. Sits and builds small towers.

9.30 M still playing with bricks, pushing them to and fro. Other children playing alongside but M takes no notice of them, even when towers fall with a noise.

9.55 Still with bricks. Approached by nursery assistant. Allows himself to be taken to milk table—no expression on face.

10.35 Playing listlessly with sand, running fingers through it. Edges away from other children.

11.00 Standing watching other children in the sand. I went over to suggest he play with Mary in the playhouse but he shrinks back. Looks towards book corner so I take him there and talk about the books. No response. Leave him there.

11.30 Still in book corner, not looking at books, rocking slightly on chair. Time for group singing and story. Allows himself to be brought into group but shrinks from physical contact and sits slightly apart.

Following this observation, Miss Smith resolved to take more positive steps to involve Martin in the classroom activities and to build up a relationship with him. Every morning she took his hand and walked around the classroom with him, commenting on the activities of the other children. She took every opportunity to talk to him as she passed him and encouraged the nursery assistant to work alongside Martin, as she herself often did, providing a running commentary on what she was doing. After two weeks, Miss Smith decided to make another sampling check to see if the view that there had been no change in Martin's behaviour was borne out.

Observation 2 30.9.74

9.15 Martin pushed through door by mother. He looks white and listless but shows no emotion as nursery assistant greets him and tries to persuade him to take off his coat. Allows his coat to be removed but takes no action himself.

10.00 Martin still playing with water, where he had been taken first. No response to other children. Pouring water mechanically from one cup to another.

10.30 Only sign of emotion when milk spilt. Momentary flinching as I approached, then impassive as milk mopped up.

11.00 Martin discovered asleep, sucking his thumb, in book corner.

11.45 Martin awoke during singing but sat in the chair, seeming to watch the group. First time I've noticed any interest.

After this observation Miss Smith had further discussion with the headteacher and they made arrangements to discuss Martin's problems together with the mother two mornings later. This resulted in a long talk during which Martin's mother described a long history of problems, desertion by the natural father, ill treatment by several other men, and finally the move to a new town to avoid the accumulated problems of the previous home. Arrangements were made for support for the mother. The welfare officer was approached and he agreed to cooperate with the social services. Meanwhile, in the classroom Miss Smith continued her positive action, trying to build an expectation for talk with Martin, both with her and with other children.

A further observation was made three weeks later.

Observation 3 22.10.74

9.05 Martin walks in and takes coat off. No change in expression when greeted by teacher but allows himself to be clad in painting overall when this is suggested.

9.30 Martin has wandered off, leaving 'painting' on easel and still with apron on. Stands watching a group building with bricks. A slight smile as tower falls?

10.00 Has been encouraged to 'join in' the activity of cleaning out the rabbit. Watches impassively but goes to get newspaper when asked.

10.30 Standing watching the children in the play house. Draws back when approached by Mary.

11.00 Playing in the sand. Engrossed in making sand pies.

11.30 Joins group for singing and rocks in time to the music.

Child study 2 Jean: 4 years 10 months

The following observations were made of Jean over the same period. She, too, never approached other children or the teacher, who now felt that an objective view should be taken to check the impression that Jean had given of being a shy, withdrawn girl.

Observation 1 16.9.74

8.50 Jean looks as though she has been crying but is now composed. Turns away from teacher but talks to mother until she leaves her settled at the clay table.

9.30 Watching other children at clay table with some horror at the mess they are making. Does not approach adult but looks relieved when it is suggested she washes her hands.

10.00 'Busy' ironing in the play house. No talking to others but sometimes stops to watch others. 'Irons' the tablecloth when nursery assistant suggests this but no reply to her questions or comments.

E

10.40   Systematically making all the jigsaws, re-
turning them to the shelf and getting another
when each is completed. Absorbed.

11.00   Looks pleased when I comment on how good
she is at making jigsaws, but says nothing.
Nods agreement to play with something
else. Nods when sand is suggested—goes
there quite happily.

11.35   Joins in rhymes and songs. Seems to listen
to story and watches reactions of other
children.

A discussion with the mother, following this,
revealed that Jean is an only child and lives in rather
an isolated house but is used to her Granny's
company, as she lives near. Mother suspected
Granny may have told her to be good and said she
would 'have a talk with Jean', and with Granny.

Observations were made again two weeks later.

Observation 2   3.10.74

9.00   Jean says goodbye to mother at the door,
takes off her coat, goes to the painting easel
and starts to paint. I approach and talk
about putting on apron. Jean nods.

9.15   Approaches nursery assistant and asks her
to keep the picture for her mummy. She
says it is a picture of mummy when asked.

9.45   Playing with jigsaws, talks to nursery
assistant about the biggest and hardest one.

10.20   Helps nursery assistant to clear used milk
mugs and goes to play house.

10.45   Still playing with doll, undressing, taking
for walk in pram. Stops to look at other
children but moves on if spoken to by them.

11.20   Absorbed in reading corner, smiles at Mary
sitting nearby. Listens when I talk to Mary
and joins in talk briefly.

Child study 3   Michael: 4 years 11 months

Michael has come from the nursery class and is said
to be 'very quiet and not talking very much'. After
two weeks his teacher decided to make observations
by the sampling method to see whether this would
bear out the view she was gaining, which seemed to
agree with that of the nursery teacher.

Observation   20.9.74

9.10   Arrived late and rushed in, saying 'Goodbye' to his mother and going straight to the
bricks, where three other boys were playing.
Said 'That's a good one' and joined in with
them.

9.35   Playing in the sand with four others. Talking
about what he was making—roads for his
car and replied to me when I asked about
car journey. Talked about holidays, motorway. Needed a lot of help but responded
adequately.

10.00   Goes for his milk from the table when this is
suggested by nursery assistant. Sits beside
Annette and compares bottles—'I've got
more than you.'

10.35   Outside on large apparatus with five boys,
racing and climbing. A lot of noise and
shouting.

11.00   Comes to writing table when this is suggested and allows himself to be shown the
best way of holding crayon. Answers my
questions and comments but does not initiate any remark.

11.30   Fidgeting in big group and poking Stephen
beside him during singing and story. Does
not appear to be listening to stories or
poems.

Martin, Jean and Michael had all been classed
as quiet children, yet the observations showed
problems of different severity.

In each case Miss Smith made a decision on the
evidence of her observations and wrote up her
comments as a basis for future action.

*What differences are indicated by the observations
and what action would you advise Miss Smith to take,
in order to give the most appropriate help to each
child?*

2 *The following summaries indicate the judgments
made by Miss Smith about the children and the action
that she was able to take. In your view, does she seem
to have acted wisely?*

Martin

Martin's teacher felt that her observations built up a picture of a child with severe emotional problems and reinforced her first impressions, which led to the discussions with the headteacher, mother and psychiatric social worker. The third observation bore out her hope that there was some slight improvement in Martin's behaviour. She felt that similar close observations would be needed to be made at regular intervals to discover whether progress was being made and what further action would need to be taken. She continued to make special efforts to talk to him frequently, to involve him in activities and to support him in making relationships with others.

Jean

This observation showed a change in Jean's behaviour over the two weeks. She now approached the nursery assistant when she needed help and showed more tolerance of other children, particularly when the teacher was present. The teacher realized there had been progress and that, although Jean still needed encouragement in talking to adults and particularly with other children, there seemed to be no reason to think that she had severe problems. It seemed likely that given time and deliberate help from the teacher in building up relationships, Jean would soon make the adjustment from the security of a quiet home to the demands of the classroom.

Michael

From her observation of Michael Miss Smith realized that he was using language a great deal with his friends and was able to answer adequately when approached by the teacher. However, he never approached the teacher himself or initiated conversation and it seemed that this unwillingness to talk spontaneously to an adult in school had given him the reputation for being a nontalker. Miss Smith realized that she would need to build up the sort of relationship with Michael in which he felt at ease with the adult and able to talk to her. She planned to make frequent efforts to talk to Michael and invite him to take part in activities with her, in order to develop a different relationship with her and encourage a different approach to adults.

Applications

Bearing in mind the points to notice as outlined on pages 56 to 58, observations might now be made of a child whom the teacher thinks is quiet and who does not seem to talk in the classroom. The picture gained of the child could then be compared with the earlier impression and plans for future action considered. Following this, all children who are found by the sampling check to use little talk in the classroom should be more closely studied.

Further reading

Books about children with particular problems usually touch only briefly on the quiet child and offer little that close observation on the part of the teacher and then the action suggested in this chapter cannot give. However, an interesting book about a child with severe emotional problems is *Dibs in Search of Self* by V. Axline. The way in which the author established a relationship with Dibs and helped him, through play therapy, to overcome his problems provides compulsive reading which might help the reader to gain a fuller understanding of the nature of problems of this kind.

AXLINE, V. (1964) *Dibs in Search of Self* Penguin

Chapter seven

Some problems in using speech

There are some problems of communication between teacher and child that arise because of difficulties the child may have in using speech. These difficulties are of two kinds.

First, there are problems caused by the child's difficulties in applying the rules which govern the production of the *structural features or forms* of speech. We will refer to the *adult speech form* as the one towards which children are progressing. The *adult speech form* with which children may be familiar, and which serves as the model from which they learn, may or may not be *correct* in terms of standard use of English. For example, the use of 'was' and 'were' is often reversed in practice. It would be unusual, however, to find adults using the form 'goed' instead of 'went', and we refer to the child's progress towards producing the *adult speech form* as his maturity in using *speech structures or forms*.

In addition to the child's problems of acquiring adult speech forms, he may still use what we will describe as *babyisms*. These are words which he may have been encouraged to use as a baby, for example, 'bye-byes' for 'sleep', 'chuff-chuff' for 'train'. Where such babyisms linger on, probably because they are encouraged by parents, the child may be hindered from developing speech naturally because he is not given adequate experiences. *Babyisms*, then, are likely to be an indication of the kind of experience of using language which is being given at home.

Second, there are problems in using speech which stem from the child's difficulties in controlling the actions of his mouth, tongue and throat in those movements which are needed to produce the different sounds and intonations which make up speech. We refer to this activity as *articulating* and

we will refer to the child's difficulties as *problems of articulation*. The child's problems of articulation may cause difficulties in communicating since they may hinder the listener from understanding what the child is saying; but it is not a difficulty of using language. The child may have adequate knowledge of language, may select the words correctly and know what he wants to say; his difficulty is in producing a pattern of sounds that will be recognized by others.

Another problem of articulation is that of controlling the flow of sounds as, for example, in stammering. Such problems cause embarrassment and frustration, both to the child and those who listen to him. Impatience on the part of the listener may only increase the child's problems of control.

The different problems we have outlined here are referred to as *problems in using speech*, since they are problems concerned with the production of speech and are not problems of using language. Difficulties of this kind are important because they hinder communication, although for the most part they are temporary, experienced to some degree by all children, and are gradually overcome as the child grows older. For a few children they present gross difficulties, which may extend long after other children have overcome their problems. If the child is not helped, such difficulties in producing speech may seriously affect his learning and so affect his achievement in later years. We will now go on to discuss each of the problems of producing speech more fully.

Maturity in the structuring of speech

Some children's talk may be difficult to understand because the structure of the speech is still immature, and in some cases because *baby* talk has been prolonged.

At two years old the child's speech can be described as *telegraphic* because the embedding, linking or supporting words of the adult form of speech are not present, so that the child's speech appears to be a reduction of the adult form. In fact the child is able to produce only those words for which there is a clear demonstration of meaning, generally those which are labels for people, objects and actions. When *telegraphic* speech is used much of the child's meaning has to be caught from other aspects of his behaviour, and indeed from the very context in which it appears. For example, the child's utterance, 'Johnnie—car' could hold any one of many possible meanings. The tone of the child's voice, his gestures, actions and facial expression, and the situation in which the utterance is used, will provide the listener with some indication of its likely meaning.

The term *telegraphic* is, in fact, not the most apt, since the child has not condensed a fuller form of his message deliberately. At two years old the words 'Johnnie—car' are the only speech elements he can produce and his stamping, crying and pointing at the culprit who has taken his car together express the meaning he intends to communicate to the adult, as he makes simultaneous physical efforts to gain attention.

By the time the child is nearing three years old the same message is likely to be conveyed in a form more like the following: 'Tom naughty—Tom got mine car—Johnnie want car—*now*', and by five years old the underlying meaning of a similar situation may be expressed in a much fuller form of message, for example: 'Tommy taked my car—that blue one over there—it's mine—and I want it because my mum might be cross if I don't take it home.'

Between the ages of two and five years old the child gradually moves from a *telegraphic* form of speech to one which is very near to the adult speech form. We can perhaps make the point more clearly by looking again at these three utterances made at different ages but in a similar situation.

Typical of two year old's talk
'Johnnie—car'

This is a two-word, telegraphic utterance. It relies mainly on gesture, intonation and other behaviour —perhaps stamping and crying—for communication and speech expresses only a part of the message.

Typical of the child's talk between the ages of two and a half and three and a half years
'Tom naughty—Tom got mine car—Johnnie want car—me want it now.'

The child uses his own name or 'me' and has not yet mastered 'I'. He confuses 'mine' and 'my' and some words are replacements for others. The complete message would read: Tom is naughty— he has got my car—I want my car—I want it now. Some words are missed out, i.e. is, has; some words are replacements for others, i.e. 'mine' for 'my', 'Johnnie' for 'I', 'me' for 'I'. One agreement is missing—Johnnie want(s).

Appearing in many children from four years of age onwards
'Tommy taked my car—that blue one over there— it's mine—and I want it because my mum might be cross if I don't take it home.'

Now the child's speech is almost mature. He has extracted the general rule that past is indicated by adding 'ed' but has not yet learned all the exceptions, for example, the irregular past tense 'took'. He uses 'because' and 'if' to link dependent statements and shows awareness that possible outcomes are not entirely predictable by using 'might'. He gives considerable information for identifying the car 'that blue one over there'.

Appraising the maturity of the child's speech
We will now summarize what might be observed when making some appraisal of the maturity of the child's speech. We can approach this best by asking a number of questions about the child's speech.

1   Is the child's speech still *telegraphic*: that is, are the child's utterances of one, two or three words, representing only a *part* of what he is trying to communicate? Must the listener seek his meaning more from his tone of voice, facial expression, gestures, and actions, than from the words he produces?

If the child's speech is more than *telegraphic* the following questions can be asked:

2   Are there still some omissions in the form of speech used? The listener can identify the kind of words which are being omitted: these are likely to be

> parts of the verb (e.g. am, is, are, was, were, has, have, had, do, does, did, will, shall)
> articles and possessives (e.g. a, the, my, your, his, her)
> prepositions (e.g. on, in, with, by, to)
> pronouns (e.g. I, you, he, somebody, who).

3   Does he fail to make agreements between subject and the verb, for example, 'Tommy want' instead of 'Tommy wants', or between articles and nouns, for example, 'a cars' or 'two car'?

4   Does he show that he is aware that time sequences can be expressed through the verb by using past and future tenses? Is he aware of regular and irregular endings? For example, he may use the regular past ending 'ed' as in 'washed' and 'climbed', and still be extending this to all verbs saying, for example, 'goed', 'runned', 'hitted', 'finded'. He may show, however, that he is aware of irregular past tenses, for example, saying, 'went' (not 'goed'), 'took' (not 'taked'), 'hit' (not 'hitted').

5   Finally we might note whether the child is using words like 'because', 'if' and 'when' to link statements which have some relationship between them or uses words that express uncertainty, for example 'perhaps', 'could' and 'might'.

The use of such words does not necessarily indicate that their meaning is properly understood but it does show that the child is adopting many features of the *adult form of speech*. Adults, of course, use many short utterances and many that are not in any way complex, and this is even more true of the child. But when the child is observed putting longer utterances together it should be noted as an indication that his knowledge of the possible structures of speech is extending.

Making some records of the extent of the child's maturity in using the structures of speech is perhaps best done again by using a diary-type entry after each period of observation. The features to remember will be jotted down as they occur. This should be expanded into a diary-type entry as soon as possible following the observation period and added to the continuous record which is being built up. We shall discuss the value of making continuous records of children's use of language in a later chapter, but notes about the child's approach to the adult form of speech should form part of the records kept.

Problems of articulation

A usual cause of unintelligible speech, and one that may or may not be associated with immaturity in the form of speech, stems from the child's difficulty in articulating particular sounds. In some cases the child's speech is not made unintelligible, but where there is gross distortion the child is likely to suffer much frustration because others cannot understand what he says to them. The problems may not be caused by the child's inability to distinguish some of the sounds he hears, but by his inability to discover the way in which the sounds are produced. In some cases the difficult sounds for the child are replaced by others, e.g. *wun* for *run*, or *fing* for *thing*. Sometimes sounds are just omitted, as in *poon* for *spoon*. Such substitutions and omissions are so usual in the speech of the young child that the listener quickly recognizes them and communication is not impaired. By the age of seven or eight the child should have outgrown all of these problems.

For most children difficulties in articulation will not make their talk unintelligible, and as long as there is evidence that a child is growing out of these difficulties steadily, there is not likely to be a serious problem for him. But even small difficulties should be noted and the child helped from time to time to produce the elusive sounds correctly. Many parents will intuitively be helping their children to master such sounds, but for others, unless the teacher offers help from time to time, the child may continue to have minor problems of articulation in later years.

The child whose difficulties in articulation are numerous and so grossly disturb his speech that others cannot understand what he is trying to say needs help as soon as possible. The help of a speech therapist may be needed and certainly the teacher should seek the advice of a speech therapist about what might be done in school. Anything that can help to reduce the problems of communication will help the child. If the teacher can be helped to interpret more easily what the child is trying to say, the child will also be helped, because at last he finds that he can communicate with someone. It is important to reduce the child's frustration without making him self-conscious, but he must also be encouraged to make efforts to overcome his difficulties. The following suggestions have been made by speech therapists for guiding the action that teachers are able to take to help the child who has articulation problems.

Identifying the problems of intelligibility

Any situation in which the child is talking gives the teacher an opportunity to discover how intelligible the child's speech is and the nature of any difficulties which impede the listener's understanding of what he says. If the teacher has not already realized that the child has difficulties of articulation, then the sampling check that we have suggested is likely to alert the teacher to the child's problem, unless he is one of those children who are not able to talk to anyone. The embarrassment and frustration associated with gross articulation difficulty may indeed become so overwhelming that the child gives up trying to communicate. For most children, however, there will be only a few sounds which cause some difficulty.

Looking at a picture book with a child is a useful way of trying to discover his problems of articulation. As he comes close enough to look at the picture he is in a position where even a low voice can be heard and the problems of listening caused by the child's movements in play situations are avoided. The pictures which have been provided for introducing the teacher to the principles of making an appraisal can be used for this purpose. The child can be asked to name objects in the pictures and a phonic representation of what he says can be written down, together with the word it represents. In this way the details of the child's problems of articu-

lation can be discovered. It is important for the teacher to recognize the problem sounds because intuitively the substitutions can then be made as the teacher listens and the child talks, and the child may be understood more easily.

Once the problems are recognized the child can be helped, first to listen to sounds and to identify the sounds he has difficulty with so we may be sure he is hearing correctly.

Pictures or objects that the child is playing with may be used to help the child indicate the correct sound, without asking him to repeat it. For example if he has problems with the sound *c* and always substitutes *t*, then pictures of objects or the objects themselves can be used. If the child is playing with a car, the teacher may say, 'What do we call this?' and point to the car, and then follow by using a wrong sound but one the child would not use, for instance, 'Is it a *par*?' with a smile and a perceptible shake of the head to help the child understand what is required. Then the child may be given the sound he would make—'Is it a *tar*?'—again he would be helped to recognize that this was wrong. Finally the child may be asked 'Is it a *car*?.' Even though he may not be able to reproduce the word correctly, it is important that he should be able to identify the correct sound. Once the child has played the game once or twice he will perhaps begin to join in readily. 'Is this a *n*up? No? Is it a *p*up? No? Is this a *t*up? No? Is it a *c*up?' wait for the 'Yes' and then emphasize 'Yes it's a *c*up.'

Other games may be played which help him to repeat the needed sounds, not in making words but in producing sounds for effect. If the child fails to produce the sound it is not then felt as a failure to produce the word, for the sound he can make may be equally suitable for the game that is played. The child is asked to think about the sounds that are made in particular situations or by animals. All children at times pretend to be hissing snakes—*sssssssss*—or bees buzzing *zzzzzzzzz*. Barking dogs can produce the sound *w* and the end sound *ff*, playing at shunting trains practises *sh sh sh*, growling bears help the child to use the back of the throat for *grrrrr*, roaring cars or aeroplane engines require the rolling *rrrr*. Pretending to use a drum is useful for the light *t-t-t-t* or heavy *boom, boom, boom* with the stress on *b* and *m*. A motorbike engine starting might be *c-c-c-c* and imitating the sounds of the cuckoo can produce the same sound. Once the teacher has identified the child's problem, situations can be invented in which the sounds the child needs can be practised. This gives the child opportunities to try to make the sounds which are difficult for him but which do not depend on producing words, and so failure is avoided because they are introduced in fun and as a bit of nonsense play.

Once the child shows he can produce the offending sounds in such games, then the teacher may help him with jingles in which nonsense words are used. Again, the whole thing should be fun and the child should be encouraged to join in without drawing attention to his speech or making him self-conscious about his problem. The main aim should be to encourage him to remain confident about talking with the teacher, so that eventually, as he is seen to be approaching mastery of the difficult sounds and he is assured of success, the teacher can begin to remind him to make special efforts with one or two of the sounds as he talks, so that his difficulties are eliminated one by one. Teachers may be interested to invent some jingles which might help children with particular articulation problems.

The child who stammers

There are different views on what causes stammering and what may be the most helpful treatment. It is normal for children of between two and five or six years of age to hesitate and repeat themselves as they search for words, or ways in which to express their ideas. Many children who stammer at this stage grow out of it. However, it is important that specialist advice should be sought where:

1 there is a history of stammering in the family
2 the child is frequently tense and the stammer is associated with signs of anxiety, or if the stammer itself has become a source of anxiety
3 the stammer is part of a pattern of behaviour, for example blushing, stamping or spasmodic movements of the face or body.

As stammering is usually less likely to occur when the child is relaxed, it would be helpful to note if there are any situations where the child stammers less. Some children may stammer less when talking in play situations, talking to pets or when speech is spontaneous and not provoked by questions.

The young child who stammers is not likely to improve if his attention is drawn to his problem. To ask him to repeat what he was trying to say is only likely to increase his anxiety. What he really needs is an indication, perhaps by the teacher sitting down beside him, that she is prepared to wait for him and will listen patiently until he has completed what he is trying to say. Once the child is relaxed and assured of the teacher's patient listening, then he may be helped by repeating jingles and rhymes in a deliberate way with his attention concentrated on trying to keep the rhythm set by the teacher.

Stammering may be a symptom of emotional problems and therefore the teacher should be particularly sensitive to the child's feelings. A relaxed, easy atmosphere with little pressure and the avoidance of situations in which everybody's attention is drawn to him as he talks, will perhaps be most helpful for the child.

The child who 'clutters' may at first sound like the one who stammers and from the teacher's viewpoint it may not be necessary to distinguish between these problems. The child stops and starts, pausing at odd places and always sounds as though he is in a hurry. The child's utterances may lack organization. This may be due to his distractability; his attention may wander from what he is trying to communicate and he will need help in concentrating on the topic in hand. He may be a child who is awkward in other movements and his problems in producing speech may stem from a more general problem of control.

A child who has this kind of problem may need help with the control of other movements and not just those associated with the production of speech, for example, tapping out a rhythm for the jingles he joins in with the teacher; deliberately having fun with the controlled intonation of sounds, with the teacher; talking about children climbing higher and higher (with the voice rising) to the top of the slide, and then coming down, down, down (with voice deepening) to the bottom.

Making an appraisal

The teacher will become aware of the child's problems in producing speech through the sampling check, if not before, and notes will be made about the way in which the child talks with others and the extent to which relationships with others are affected by his difficulties in communicating.

It will then be necessary to arrange some situation in which the teacher can talk with the child in order to discover the details of his problems of articulation or of observing the rules of ordering speech. If the teacher is to identify and remember the child's problems, then notes about what is discovered must be jotted down, perhaps on a tear-off notepad. As soon as possible after such observations the teacher should summarize what has been discovered and enter the findings as part of a continuing record.

Children who have problems of this kind will need regular and frequent help for short periods and each encounter can provide some pointers to the progress the child is making. Looking back over the continuing record should then help the teacher to see whether the child is mastering his problem and to reflect on what further help the child may need. Such encounters and records would not ignore other aspects of the child's use of language—any encounter should provide the opportunity to make observations of all three aspects of language use that we have defined. An example of part of a continuous record is given below. It has been written up from notes jotted down whilst working with the child. The entries that have been made are from observations of the aspects of language use we have so far discussed.

Johnnie Smith	*Birth date* 6.6.72
Observation 1	September 10th, 1975
Situation	Playing with small toys—talking with me.
Intelligibility	Generally fairly clear. Lisps and drawls, *th* for *s* and *w* for *r*.
Speech form	Uses some baby words—puffer, gee gee, handies, me-me.
	Uses either Johnnie or me—does not use 'I' at all, uses 'mine' for 'my'. Words omitted, e.g. 'I going' Omits agreement, e.g. 'car go'. Produces some longish utterances, for example, to me, 'Me going take puffer home my house.'
Observation 2	October 6th, 1975
Intelligibility	Less drawling—more alert in talking. Can make *ss* when playing 'hissing snakes' but not used in talk yet. Can roll *rr* when playing cars and makes effort in speech on some occasions.
Speech form	Generally uses 'my' and 'mine' correctly now. Asks questions, e.g. 'Why you give Tom pencil?' Still a few omissions. Is using 'because', e.g. 'Going to get my bike 'cos it's raining.'
Observation 3	December 3rd, 1975
Intelligibility	Johnnie has made great progress. Is talking readily both with children and adults. Speech is almost free of articulation problems and is now quite clear.
Speech form	Still has some problems with past tenses, but now uses 'I' and not 'me'. Few babyisms now. Using 'if' but without its meaning. Some longer utterances now.

It can be seen from the record that the teacher is building up a picture of Johnnie's difficulties which is likely to be considerably more detailed than if she had not attempted to make observations and build up a continuous record.

We would not expect any assessment to be made of the maturity of speech forms or of articulation problems; it is enough for the teacher to get a picture of each child's problems in using speech so that any difficulties might be identified and so that time spent with him can be used to help him to overcome them.

Conclusion

Listening to children talking will reveal that some three year olds, and even more four and five year olds, have speech which apart from isolated 'errors' or minor problems of articulation or pronunciation is very close to the adult speech form although, naturally, the content will be childlike. Future observations of these children can be entirely devoted to considering the way in which talk is used, that is, the teacher can now concentrate on discovering the kind of information, the kind of thought that the children's talk expresses.

Some children will reveal immaturity which is typical of the age group, and for them encouragement and frequent opportunities to talk with the teacher, sometimes to repeat sounds or words or rhymes in short spontaneous snatches with the teacher, will promote further development of speech. Observations of the kind outlined here should be made from time to time until the teacher is assured that the child's speech is maturing steadily.

Some children may have more serious difficulties: immaturity in the form of the child's speech may be evidence of general immaturity in the development of language and the teacher will need to consider what the likely causes are. The following points should be noted:

1 Mental retardation is the chief cause of gross immaturity in the development of speech; in this case other aspects of development would also be affected. Another cause of problems in developing speech is brain damage of some kind, and in these cases there may or may not be associated retardation in other areas. Some children may be retarded in speech development because they have had inadequate experiences of speech. It is important to identify such children and to concentrate on helping them develop speech forms as quickly as possible.

2 One cause of retardation that should be considered is slight hearing loss. This may prevent the child from hearing all the sounds so that he is unable to imitate them. Whereas content words are generally stressed, the embedding features, word endings and agreements may be missed. Such problems of hearing loss are also likely to account for articulation difficulties; since the child may not hear some sounds distinctly he will not produce them himself.

3 Speech immaturity might result where two languages are being used in the home. This can be confusing for the young child and make it difficult for him to extract the essential features of speech of either language. The teacher can discuss the problem with parents, suggesting that care is taken to use the different language consistently in very different situations so that the child is not confused by frequent changes.

4 Immaturity in structuring speech may also result from too great a dependence on other children for stimulation. For example, twins may be retarded in language development because they are seen as company for each other and so are not given adequate experience of the adult form of speech. The teacher can discuss such problems with parents, so that a deliberate effort can be made at home, and at school, to involve them separately in talk with adults.

5 A child whose mother or older brothers and sisters always anticipate his needs may not be stimulated to speak much and if baby talk is always used when talking to him he will always be given immature forms as his model. The child cannot learn to structure speech on the adult form unless he is given adequate experience from which to extract the regular features. Again it will be important to discuss the child's prob-

lems with the parents so that they might make efforts to give the child better experiences at home. In school the teacher can deliberately stimulate him to make efforts to use language more energetically.

In all cases where the form of the child's speech seems generally immature for his age, the teacher will need to decide what kind of help the child needs and what is likely to be the best source of advice for both mother and teacher. The teacher should not hesitate to try and gain professional help for any child whose problems do not begin to decrease once specific help is being given him in the classroom.

It is clear that the teacher needs to be very sensitive to the child's feelings. If his problem is dealt with in such a way that it concentrates the attention of everybody on him then he is likely to be embarrassed and his difficulty will be increased by making him very self-conscious.

On the other hand, if the child is left without help his difficulty is likely to develop into an even greater problem for him at a later stage. When the child has a gross speech difficulty the teacher should not hesitate in seeking specialist help. In the meantime, the child's problems should be discussed with the parents and some time should be spent in trying to identify the difficulties so that the teacher might understand his talk better and give support to his efforts to communicate.

Finally, we would make the point that the problems we have discussed in this and the previous chapter are all related to using speech. They are not necessarily due to lack of development in language, although each may lead to difficulties in communicating with others. The child whose speech is still telegraphic clearly has still a considerable way to go in developing language, but the child who has problems of articulation may have good resources of language and so be continually frustrated because others cannot understand him. The child who is shy and withdrawn may also have good resources of language, but be unable to talk and communicate with others because of difficulties in establishing relationships.

However, children may have none of the problems in the production of speech, but may have learned to use language for a restricted range of purposes. They may talk readily but their use of language may be limited to a few purposes which demand little thought and reflection.

Nor should we give the impression that children who have one kind of problem will not have the other. Children who have problems in producing speech may also be restricted in the purposes for which they use language. The problems are not necessarily associated though they frequently are.

Explorations

Speech difficulties

Children with speech difficulties

Miss V has identified four children in her class who have speech difficulties of some kind. She wonders what she can do to help each. Her descriptions of their problems is given below.

Peter

Peter is four and a half and has been in school for a few weeks. He is a big, plump boy but rather timid and clings to his mother. His mother is in her forties and is overprotective. She waits on him and dresses him and does not let him out of her sight except when she leaves him in school. Peter's speech is drawling and unclear and there are several sounds he is unable to make. In addition, he uses many babyisms, for example 'chuff-chuff' for 'train', 'me' for 'I', 'din-din' for 'dinner', 'handies' for 'hands'. The total effect on his speech makes it difficult for anyone to understand him. He turns frequently to the teacher for support but she is not sure what she should do to help him.

Stephen

Stephen is five and a half and has been in school for two terms. He has extreme problems of articulation and the only person in school who can understand what he says is his older brother. Stephen gets very frustrated when people cannot understand what he wants. He shouts, goes red in the face and stamps and is frequently very aggressive. He is a bright boy and makes very detailed drawings of ships, aeroplanes and horses. Miss V has discovered several of the sounds he has difficulty with. He substitutes *a* as in *bad* for *e* as in *bed*. The throaty sounds *k* and *g* are replaced by *t* and *d*; he cannot produce *r* and *th* which are replaced by *w* and *f*.

Mark

Mark has a pronounced stammer which causes him considerable embarrassment, so much so that he hardly ever speaks to anyone. He sits and plays alone and seems lethargic and wistful, avoiding contact and the need to talk.

Jenny

Jenny is very difficult to understand because she has a somewhat bizarre manner of speaking. She speaks very quickly at times and seems to leave out some initial consonants in words. She is very easily distracted and clumsy and tends to flit about the room, never settling to anything. Miss V is very worried and feels Jenny disrupts the whole class.

1 *Consider the problems of the children described. What steps should Miss V be advised to take in each case?*

In which cases should Miss V immediately try to find specialist help and in which should she perhaps first try to help the child herself, to see how he progresses?

What should Miss V say to the parents of these children and what further information about each child should she ask for when she talks to the parents?

How could Miss V set about helping each child in school?

2 *Consider Stephen's articulation problems. Can the*

reader invent a game with sounds and some jingles that Miss V could use to help Stephen?

Applications

Teachers could now identify any children in their own classes who have problems in speech. The sampling check should help. Each child's problems should then be considered very carefully and plans for helping each, as indicated in the chapter, should be made.

A picture book can be used to identify the sounds that are too difficult for the child to produce. Then sound games and jingles could be invented to help the child make efforts to overcome his problems. Any jingles used with the child should be simple enough for him to be successful in saying them. For instance, if a child needs practice in producing the sound *p*, then it would be better to use a simple sentence like, 'Peas in the pan go pop, pop, pop,' rather than 'Peter Piper picked a peck of pickled peppers.'

PART THREE

The appraisal of children's
use of language

Chapter eight

Children's use of language

Introduction

We now come to the third and last part of the guide. In part two we examined children's problems in using speech. As we have explained, these problems are not problems of language development, although they may be associated with problems of this kind. Language development is concerned with the child's growing ability to use the language system for conveying meaning. Problems in using speech may prevent communication between the child and others, but they do not necessarily mean that the child has not acquired knowledge of the language system.

The importance of language is that it allows ideas and information to be transmitted from person to person. Language provides the medium through which thinking can be expressed and, as we have argued earlier, the very use of language and the continuous experience of being amongst users of language, influences not only the way in which the child will use language, but more important, the way in which he will think, and the kind of interpretation he will make of his experiences.

Essentially, in making an appraisal of the child's use of language we are wanting to look at the kind of meanings that he is able to express through the use of language. And this is where the most important part of our task begins. How can we discriminate between the different meanings that are reflected in the child's talk? And when different meanings can be discriminated, how can we discover the range of meanings for which the child is using language?

In this final part of the guide we shall first discuss a classification of the uses of language which we hope will help teachers to observe children's talk

with a new awareness of the complexities of meaning which the child's talk demonstrates.

Becoming familiar with a new and extensive classification is not easy. In the following chapter, we shall suggest a method of exploring the use of the classification which will at the same time offer interesting and beneficial experiences to children and give the teacher opportunities to view the child's use of language.

We shall then go on to discuss how the teacher might use the classification to make written appraisals of children's use of language and to build a continuous record which can advise the teacher about the kind of experiences that might be planned to help the child.

Finally, the possibilities of making appraisals of children's use of language during ongoing classroom activities is discussed. We end by anticipating the insight that such appraisals will bring to the teacher's deliberate planning of classroom activities, so that skills of communication will be best promoted.

We have in our earlier discussions shown that young children have a potential for learning to use language, but what does that mean in terms of what children can actually *do* with language? We are interested in this question not because we expect to use language for instructing the child: we know that the young child has not yet acquired a basis of experience, or a basis for thinking, which would make that appropriate.

We have based our arguments about the importance of language in learning during the early years on the results of a research project which was undertaken by Joan Tough at the Institute of Education, University of Leeds. In this study, groups of children were selected from different home environments: one where parents had had higher education and followed professional occupations, and one where parents had had the minimum period of education and followed unskilled or semiskilled manual occupations. The different experiences of education and work, it was argued, were likely to mean that parents would provide different learning experiences for their young children, particularly different experiences of using language. In examining samples of the language produced by these groups of children from these contrasting environments, in standard play situations, at the ages of three, and in interviews using a standard set of materials at five and seven years old, clear differences emerged between the two groups of children in the way in which they were disposed to use language. There were differences in the frequency of the use of particular linguistic features, in the length of utterances and in the complexity of structure, but there were also important differences in the purposes for which language was used.

The analysis of the language used by children from the educationally-advantaged home environments promoted insights into the nature of the learning which can go on during these early years of childhood, and into the reasons why the child's experiences in using language are so important.

In order to illustrate the points we wish to make, we give below a conversation between two three and a half year old boys.

Three year olds talking

Micky and James are playing with a collection of small toys and bricks. (Micky M: James J)

1 J: Putting the sail on this boat—it's come off again—it won't stay on.

2 M: I know, get some gluey stuff—that'll make it stay on.

3 J: It's in the hole—it's on now. It's sailing down the river—that's going to be the river bank.

4 M: I'll make the river longer, shall I?

5 J: No, I want to—no, leave it—I want to, not you, it's mine.

6 M: Well, I can too. I'm getting some flat ones to go there—'cos I'm playing as well.

7 J: Make it good, then—flat—down there—so the boats can go on.

8 M: I've been on a boat and it was a very big one—and I climbed up to the top—but not right to the top. You couldn't go there—only the captain could go there.

9 J: You know, my grandad fell off a boat—he told me. And he fell in the water and grandma threw a rope, to pull him.

10 M: My boat's going under the bridge—and there's another boat coming under—and they're going to bump.

11 J: And my grandad hurt his arm—

12 M: Watch out, James, they're bumping—and everything's going in the water. Everything.

13 J: And an aeroplane comes and drops all bombs on it. On the docks and everywhere. Boom—boom—boom! Down on the ships.

14 M: No it's not—the men are getting out and up the water—and they'll shoot the aeroplane.

15 J: I'm going swimming with my dad, I am, and I'm going where it's deep, 'cos I can swim with things on my arms. I might go when my dad comes.

In this excerpt we can see that much of the young child's talk is a running commentary on his actions, almost as though he is telling himself just what he is doing. James at 1 talks in this way, almost to himself, and again at 3 he uses talk almost to guide and concentrate his actions as he pushes the mast into the hole. Language here is being used for *monitoring*, *directing* and *controlling* the child's own actions. Micky at 2 perhaps is indicating his recognition of the problem of making the mast stay upright, and anticipates a possible solution.

James begins to set up an *imaginary scene* through the use of language. The river exists only through the words that tell us (at 3) what the flat bricks, which are being laid out on the table, represent.

Micky begins to enter into the imaginative play and at 4 indicates his intended action. But there is an interruption as James tries to assert his rights to plan the river, since it was his idea. Micky, at 6, also tries to assert himself and gives a justification for his action. At this point, both children use language to maintain their rights; we refer to this as *self-maintaining* use of language. Then Micky presents a *justification* for his self-maintaining approach and so James agrees to concede his rights. Both boys seem to recognize they have equal rights to use materials which actually belong to neither of them. These children are almost at the point of using language to express a *principle* of behaviour. Doing this may not mean that the children observe the principle in practice but it is interesting that they see giving such justifications to their three year old companion as needed and appropriate.

At 7 James makes concessions to Micky, but as though to make up for this, he begins to instruct Micky about how the river must be made.

At this point it seems that the play activity reminds Micky of some earlier event and he uses language to *report* on some of his past experience, almost as though he has a picture in view which he describes.

James, as though not to be outdone, also recalls an incident, but in this case it seems he is not reporting on some scene that he remembers but on some scene that he has been told about. His grandfather's talk about the incident has been used as though it were an experience in its own right, and James is able to report on the incident which he has experienced through words alone.

James appears to be talking to Micky, but we can see that Micky goes on with his own play, *anticipating* actions and intentions. James hardly seems to have noticed that Micky is not listening and continues with his secondhand account.

At 12 Micky begins to use language to extend the imaginative scene, James joins in, helping to develop the ideas. Both boys report on the actions of the boats and the men that they are imagining. Finally, at 15 James looks into the future and *anticipates possibilities*: he even shows something very near to logical reasoning as he explains why it is suitable for him to go into the deep end at the swimming baths.

In this short excerpt from a longer recording, we can see that a number of ways of using language appear. Language is used for:

1 *Self-maintaining*—maintaining the rights and

property of the self.
2 *Directing* the child's own activity and that of others.
3 *Reporting* on present and past experience.
4 *Logical reasoning.*
5 *Predicting and anticipating possibilities.*
6 *Projecting into the experiences of others.*
7 *Building up an imaginative scene for play through talk.*

The conversation which, we can see, has a content at the level of understanding and interest of these two boys, perhaps is not of much significance in itself. The kind of thinking that they are engaged in and the use they make of language for expressing their ideas through speech reflect important skills that are developing.

In the research referred to earlier, several of the uses of language that are listed above were found most frequently in the talk of children from the educationally-advantaged homes. The talk of the children from an educationally-disadvantaged home was most frequently concerned with reporting on present experiences, at a level which we refer to as *labelling*, since the child identifies objects and actions. For example, 'That's a boat and that's its sail. There's the man and he's on the boat.'

The contrast between the use of language by the two groups of children suggested that an examination of the kind of skills that children from the advantaged homes develop would indicate the potential that young children have for using language. Children learn as a result of their own experiences. Therefore it was argued that those children who have developed a wide range of uses of language have developed them through their experiences of using language in the home. By inference then, those children who are not disposed to use language for a wide range of purposes, reflecting different ways of thinking, may not have met the kind of experiences which lead to this development. In chapter three we discussed the differences in children's use of language which seemed likely to emerge from their different experiences of using language in the home.

The conclusion from the research was not that disadvantaged children had an inadequate knowledge of language (although for some this may be the case), but that they had met insufficient experiences of language being used in certain ways, so that they were unfamiliar with some ways of thinking and therefore were not disposed to adopt these ways of thinking and uses of language themselves.

The children in both groups used language readily at each age studied. All children used language for self-maintaining and for reporting on present experiences. The disadvantaged child did not readily offer justifications for his self-maintaining behaviour as did the advantaged child, nor did he refer readily to details when reporting, or make comparisons, or sequence events: his reporting did not take on the character of analysis.

The disadvantaged child showed less inclination to use language for reporting explicitly on past experiences, for logical reasoning, for anticipating and predicting the outcome of events, for surveying possibilities or alternative courses of action or possible results and consequences, for recognizing problems and reflecting on solutions or for projecting into the lives and feelings of others and into situations which they have not experienced. The disadvantaged children did not use language readily for building up a scene through words for their imaginative play.

Since all the children in the advantaged groups readily used language for those purposes, and since the disadvantaged group had not a markedly different measured intelligence at the age of three, it seems likely that they would have developed such uses had they met them.

We might ask how important is it that children should develop such uses of language. If we consider the kind of learning that is expected of children in school we can see that the uses which did not appear to be readily available to the disadvantaged children are precisely those which are needed in school in particular learning activities.

All learning is in some way based on analysis, either of actions and movements in learning new physical skills, for example in writing; or in the close examination of aspects of the present experience, for example in building the skills of reading and looking at maps or diagrams; or in observing physical phenomena, for example in examining plants, or observing the properties of objects in water. There has to be active monitoring of the experience in order to make sense of it. Without an inclination to examine situations in this way and to express recognition of the relevant aspects, the child is not likely to make appropriate responses.

Again, all education at later stages would seem to be dependent on being able to use past experiences. That is, past experiences must be readily available for drawing relevant knowledge into the present experience. If children are not disposed to do this then their own important resources of knowledge and experiences are neglected and they fail to make the responses that are needed and expected.

Logical thinking and problem solving would seem necessary if children are to learn anything of mathematics and sciences, as well as being necessary underlying skills for carrying out practical creative work. Studies arising from the environment depend on similar skills and also on the ability to project into the lives and experiences of other people.

Using language for imaginative excursions, creating experiences as it were, is not just a skill which enhances children's play; it would seem that history and literature and the child's own creative efforts in writing are dependent on ways of thinking that are similar in character to those being developed in imaginative play by advantaged children. Imaginative thinking is needed if the child is to succeed in understanding and responding to these areas of the curriculum.

The curriculum at different stages of education can be analysed in terms of the kinds of thinking upon which subject studies are based. Such an analysis would highlight the importance of different kinds of thinking and the disadvantage of children who were not disposed to think in those ways would then become apparent. Yet these skills begin to develop in the early years before school and in the first years of school. Those children who fail to develop these skills during these years may be at particular disadvantage when they move further up the school, for it is not only that the child has not learned appropriate skills, but that he has well established attitudes which operate against him acquiring these skills later on.

How can we recognize whether children are

developing uses of language that are relevant for the tasks of learning that are presented to them in school? Before we can begin to discover this, it is necessary to establish a classification of the uses of language, so that we might have some framework to help us to discern the uses of language as children talk, and so that we might check on the child's development of the essential range of thinking skills and uses of language. A classification of the uses of language, which many teachers have found to be relevant and helpful, is set out below. The reader should refer to this during the following discussion.

The classification is one developed and used by Joan Tough: a fuller account of the research, and of the theoretical basis of the classification can be found in *The Development of Meaning: A Study of Children's Use of Language.*

Use of language

1 Self-maintaining *Instrumetal*

Strategies

1 Referring to physical and psychological needs and wants
2 Protecting the self and self interests
3 Justifying behaviour or claims
4 Criticising others
5 Threatening others

2 Directing *Regulatory*

Strategies

1 Monitoring own actions
2 Directing the actions of the self
3 Directing the actions of others
4 Collaborating in action with others

3 Reporting on present and past experiences *Personal*

Strategies

1 Labelling the components of the scene
2 Referring to detail (e.g. size, colour, and other attributes)
3 Referring to incidents
4 Referring to the sequence of events
5 Making comparisons
6 Recognizing related aspects
7 Making an analysis using several of the features above
8 Extracting or recognizing the central meaning
9 Reflecting on the meaning of experiences, including own feelings

4 Towards logical reasoning* *Heuristic*

Strategies

1 Explaining a process

2 Recognizing causal and dependent relationships
3 Recognizing problems and their solutions
4 Justifying judgments and actions
5 Reflecting on events and drawing conclusions
6 Recognizing principles

5 Predicting*

Strategies

1 Anticipating and forecasting events
2 Anticipating the detail of events
3 Anticipating a sequence of events
4 Anticipating problems and possible solutions
5 Anticipating and recognizing alternative courses of action
6 Predicting the consequences of actions or events

6 Projecting* *Interactional*

Strategies

1 Projecting into the experiences of others
2 Projecting into the feelings of others
3 Projecting into the reactions of others
4 Projecting into situations never experienced

7 Imagining* *Imaginary*

1 Developing an imaginary situation based on real life
2 Developing an imaginary situation based on fantasy
3 Developing an original story

*Strategies which serve *directing*, *reporting* and *reasoning* may serve these uses also.

The classification of the uses of language given on page 80 is based on a number of broad categories of language use. A number of strategies that serve each category are listed and they are the means by which the child reveals the purpose of his talk, for example by making a comparison, or referring to a cause and effect relationship.

The *strategies*, however, are not necessarily exclusive to one use of language. For example, the strategies listed under *reporting* can serve other uses of language. *Reporting* seems to provide the basis from which all other uses can develop.

The uses of language should not be seen as representing a developmental sequence. The child's earliest efforts to use language seem to be self-maintaining, directing and reporting. Predicting, projecting, imagining, and reasoning make a later appearance. But development within each category proceeds and it is the strategies selected that indicate the complexity of thinking that the child is trying to express. Less complex uses might be expected to appear before more complex uses, but within each broad category of language use, there are simple strategies and more complex ones. Development should be recognized *within* uses of language as well as *between* uses of language. Logical reasoning would seem to have a potential for expressing more complex thinking than reporting, but even so some strategies of reporting will appear later than some strategies of reasoning. For example, 'I want my coat because it's cold outside' does not necessarily reflect more complex thinking than, 'My coat's the one that's got a buckle, with a clasp like a snake, and a quilted lining.' The first example may be judged as reasoning and the second as reporting but no developmental or hierarchical relationship necessarily exists between them.

The child uses language not only to give information to his listeners but also to seek information from them by asking questions. How, then, can we make an appraisal of this disposition to ask questions?

We will need perhaps to refer to the kind of questions asked quite separately. We cannot say, for example, that asking the question 'Why?' is always evidence of logical reasoning, or that 'How?'

questions are evidence of reporting. But we can note the kind of information that particular kinds of questions invite and so the kind of experience for the child that might follow. We can analyse questions within the framework on the basis of the kind of use of language they anticipate.

The classification of the uses of language provides us with a basis for making appraisals of the child's use of language. It may be difficult to place some of the language used by children within the classification, but it makes it possible to make some analysis while observing children's talk. Once the classification is familiar and is established, skill in using it should enable the teacher to make an analysis of the child's use of language as she talks with him.

We should perhaps point out that sometimes utterances will not fit clearly within one use of language but may seem to belong to more than one. This is not important. Recognizing that it has characteristics of more than one use is the important thing and the most complex aspect is perhaps the one that should be noted. It is important to remember that the classification is there to help us recognize and describe what the child is doing as he uses language and is not likely to remove all the problems of identification.

Teachers may find that it takes a little time before the various aspects of the classification are fully appreciated. Those teachers who have worked with it and followed our suggestions for making appraisals, found the more familiar they became with applying the classification, the more they appreciated the value of their new skill and the insights that it brought them.

The reader is asked to remember, then, that although the classification may appear to be a formidable list of uses, it is only a framework given as a guide to help teachers identify uses of language which they are probably already fostering, either intuitively, or with some deliberation.

Set out on pages 82 to 85 is the classification giving examples of each strategy so that it may serve as a framework for discussion and illustrate the kinds of thinking that might be distinguished as they are expressed in children's talk.

A classification of the uses of language with examples

Uses of language and strategies	In present experience
1 Self-maintaining	
1 Referring to physical and psychological needs and wants	1 I want my milk now Watch me, watch what I can do
2 Protection of the self and of self interests	2 You're hurting me. Go away Will you give me it, it's mine
3 Justifying behaviour or claims	3 I'm hitting him because he spoiled my picture I can have it 'cos I asked first
4 Criticising others	4 I don't like your building, it's silly
5 Threatening others	5 If you don't give me that car I'll hit you
2 Directing	
1 Monitoring own actions	1 Turning it round, the lorry's going round
2 Directing the actions of the self	2 Turn it—it's hard—turn it a bit—a bit and take it off like that. Now the wheel—careful it should fit—a bit further round—that's it
3 Directing the actions of others	3 You take your lorry over there and put a load on it and then push it hard down this hill
4 Collaborating in action with others	4 You cut the paper and I'll stick it and we'll put it on there for an aeroplane
3 Reporting	*(Arising out of play situation)*
1 Labelling the components of the scene	1 That's a car, there's a bus and that's a lorry
2 Referring to detail (e.g. size, colour and other attributes)	2 That little red bus has a little door at the back that opens
3 Referring to incidents	3 That boy's got some bricks, he's piling them up but Jim's knocking them down again
4 Referring to the sequence of events	4 He's put a load on and he's taking it over to the building and then it crashes
5 Making comparisons	5 This lorry is bigger than the red bus but it's the same colour
6 Recognizing related aspects	6 When it goes fast it crashes so the bricks fall out
7 Making an analysis using several of features above	7 There's three little lorries and two big ones but they won't all go in the garage, and that one's too big, it'll have to stay outside
8 Extracting or recognizing the central meaning	8 We're pretending it's an accident
9 Reflecting on the meaning of experiences, including own feelings	9 I like playing with lorries but I don't like that boy banging mine—he's spoiling it

From past experience	*In imagined context

From past experience

1 I wanted to play and John wouldn't let me
   Didn't you come to see me swimming

2 I told the teacher about you

3 I didn't mean to hurt him

4 You were very naughty yesterday.
   I didn't like you

5 I told him I'd hit him if he touched my bike
   and he did

***In imagined context**

1 Get away *I'm* putting the fire out

2 I'm the captain of this boat and I don't want
   you to sail on it

3 I'm the driver so *I've* got to come in front

4 You're a weedy soldier you can't kill a giant

5 Don't come up here. I'll kill you with my
   sword

1 Pouring out the tea, one on there, one on there
   and one on there

2 I'm a princess and I've to fasten this brooch
   on my cloak—push it through—it's hard to
   push—there it's fastened

3 You fetch the ladder and climb up to the fire
   to put it out

4 Let's put the plank out. I'll hold it. You get
   the pirate and we'll send him on it

(Jenny talking of a visit to her aunt's)

1 My aunty has a cat and a budgie

2 Her beds were on top and underneath and
   there was a little ladder

3 I rolled off my bed onto the floor

4 We got on the bus and then a train and
   Uncle Dick met us when we got there

5 It wasn't as comfortable as my bed

6 The bus was late and we had to run to catch
   the train

7 There were two beds and one was on top of
   the other and you'd to climb a little ladder to
   get up on it

8 It wasn't a holiday really. My dad went to
   help Uncle Dick

9 It's nice at my aunty's but I wouldn't like to
   stay there for ever

(Making a story about a painting)

1 There's a witch and that's her cat

2 And she's putting a pointed hat on

3 The cat is scratching the man with its sharp claws

4 And the witch gets on the broomstick and then
   the cat jumps on and they fly away

5 Her cat's bigger than a real one and it's got
   long claws

6 And she goes high in the air and the world
   looks little

7 She can see the people far away and there's
   fields and some cows and there's a lot of trees
   with a flat place in the middle to land on

8 And a witch is magic and she's doing all
   things we can't do

9 And she's a nice witch really. Nice witches do
   good things, not bad things

A classification of uses of language with examples (cont.)

Uses of language and strategies	In present experience
4 Towards logical reasoning	
1 Explaining a process	1 When you break your arm they put something on it like a bandage and plaster, all over
2 Recognizing causal and dependent relationships	2 If the bridge is low, boats can't go under and it will have to open in the middle to let them go through
3 Recognizing problems and their solutions	3 This box isn't big enough to make a garage so I'm going to make it with blocks
4 Justifying judgments and actions	4 I'm cutting this box to make doors 'cos we need doors to put the cars in
5 Reflecting on events and drawing conclusions	5 I don't think we'd better take the clock to pieces, we couldn't put it back again
6 Recognizing principles	6 I want a bike but I can't have one because it's too dangerous on our road
5 Predicting	**From immediate situation**
1 Anticipating/forecasting	1 I'm going to paint a picture when I've finished my milk
2 Anticipating the detail of actions and events	2 I'm going to make some tarts with jam in, some red and some yellow ones
3 Anticipating a sequence of events	3 I'm going to put some more bricks on that tower and then I'll put this flag on and it'll all come crashing down
4 Anticipating problems and possible solutions	4 That brick won't be long enough to go over the road, I'll go and find a piece of wood
5 Anticipating and recognizing alternative courses of action	5 We could make a bridge over with a box or we could have a long rope or get a ladder
6 Predicting consequences of actions or events	6 That propeller will fall off if you can't stick it on properly
6 Projecting	
1 Projecting into the experiences of others	1 He's driving fast in his car and it'll be all windy and cold and he hasn't got a coat on
2 Projecting into feelings of others	2 I think he's frightened his mother will be cross
3 Projecting into reactions of others	3 He'll come and get all the bricks back if we take them
4 Projecting into situation never experienced	4 That boy spilt all the red paint and he doesn't like cleaning it up I wouldn't like to be a rabbit living in that cage, would you?
*7 Imagining	Many examples have been quoted in the fourth column throughout

From past experience

1 I made a puppet at home. I made it with a paper bag and I cut a mouth and some eyes so I could put my hand in to make it act like a clown
2 I put my boat in the pond but the wind blew it over so it sunk
3 I broke my aeroplane and I didn't have any glue so I'd to stick it with Sellotape
4 I didn't want to go out because I hadn't finished my drawing
5 All that rain came and that's why it's muddy

6 Cars can't go in floods but boats can

Beyond immediate situation

1 My dad's going to London and he's going to go on a fast train
2 We're going to get a hamster and it will have to have a cage with a wheel
3 I'm going on a bus like that to see my Grandma after she comes out of hospital
4 You can't get the man out of the sea with an aeroplane, you'll have to get a helicopter
5 You'll have to climb the steps to get to the top of the tower but you could go up in the lift
6 If you drive to the top of the cliff and you don't stop you'll go whizzing down to the sea

1 There was all mud in the field and the man got stuck and that was horrible
2 He didn't know how to get out and he was frightened

3 I'm going to help my dad tonight and I think he'll buy me some sweets
4 It's hot in the desert and I think you'll get sand blowing all over you

Examples of imagining have been drawn from three different contexts

*In imagined context

1 I'm the mummy and I've put a teabag in and we'll have to boil the water and make some tea

2 You haven't put any sugar in so it's not very nice tea
3 I'm cleaning up the house but there isn't a vac so I'll have to use this brush
4 I'm putting all the little girl's things away 'cos she's poorly in bed
5 She'll have to stay in bed and I think she'll get poorly and the doctor will come and that will be very bad
6 You're the daddy and you'll have to go to work 'cos daddies do

1 The man's going to come along the road

2 He's going to put a fence round and then put the cows inside. He'll need a stick
3 That dog will bark and chase the cows over the road and then they'll get lost
4 If they get lost the farm dog will go out and find them and bring them back
5 The cows could stay on the farm or they could go in the fields or the farmer might take them to market
6 When the farmer's been to market there'll be no animals left on the farm

1 The baddies will go to prison and it'll be all dark and cold
2 The little boy wanted his mummy but the baddies took him away and he was frightened and he cried
3 The policeman will put all the baddies in prison if they take people like that
4 It won't be nice in prison with bars on the windows and locked in

an imagined context based on real life
an imagined context based on fantasy
developing an original story

In making an appraisal of the child's use of language, it is the content of the child's talk, the kind of information with which he deals, and the manner in which he deals with it, that is important. This is familiar ground for any teacher: sometimes with complete awareness and deliberation, but for the most part perhaps quite intuitively, the child is helped to extend his thinking and learning as the teacher talks with him. This can be done by asking questions, listening and commenting on what he says, in an effort to draw from him what he knows.

Conclusion

The teacher helps him to formulate ideas, examine relationships, reflect and reason about what he experiences, and consider the viewpoint of other people. Teachers generally encourage the use of language for these purposes because it is felt that this helps the child to think and learn. The child is also encouraged to use his imagination and to pursue ideas in a particularly individual way. These are the uses of language which teachers and some children are employing all the time, but only when we set them out in some kind of classification do we begin to appreciate the full complexity of the activity of talking.

Explorations

The uses of language

1 Spot the uses

Here are seven excerpts from tape recordings of children talking in school. In each example most of the talk belongs to *one* of the main uses of language which form the classification. Each example illustrates one of the following uses:

1 Self-maintaining
2 Directing
3 Reporting
4 Reasoning
5 Predicting
6 Projecting
7 Imagining

Consider each example and decide to which of the uses listed above most of the child's talk belongs.

Conversation 1

Jason on the climbing frame. (Jason J: Teacher T)

1 J: I'm holding on very tight, because I might fall off if I don't hold tight. If you fall off the ambulance comes to take you to the hospital because you're hurt.

2 T: Do you know someone who had to go to hospital, Jason?

3 J: Yes. Stephen went to hospital, big Stephen, because he fell when he was climbing in a house. My mummy says I haven't got to go there in those new houses because it's dangerous and you could break your leg or crack your head.

4 T: Is that what Stephen did?

5 J: Yes he broke his leg so they had to put a plaster on to keep it straight. If they didn't it wouldn't mend properly. But he's lucky really, 'cos he could have killed himself and that would be worse.

Conversation 2

Wanda talking about pets on the farm. (Wanda W: Teacher T)

1 W: And do you know? There's Barney and she's only got three legs. She was out somewhere and she was caught in a trap. She's only little, not as big as our other dog.

2 T: Oh, dear.

3 W: And she's only got three legs. And when we're away to bed she goes up to Robin's knee and then she puts her head down and soon she goes to sleep.

4 T: That's a nice comfortable bed, isn't it?

5 W: Yes. And she's got a wee cat and it's called Snowball because he's so white. And he's nice and furry and you see I've got a wee bell with a thing round it and I can take it out of this here and roll it and then he runs after it and jumps on it. He's such a nice wee cat. I wish he'd stay little always.

Conversation 3

Andrew and his horse. (Andrew A: Teacher T)

1 A: He's been a long way, now. He wants something to eat.

2 T: What would he like to eat?

3 A: Some oats. Have you got a bag for him to eat his oats from?

4 T: A nose bag, yes I think we have something that will do. (provides a paper carrier bag)

5 A: Yes that will do. Here you are horse. (looping the handles round horse's ears)

6 T: Does your horse need a drink?

7 A: Yes . . . I'll go to the magic wishing well here it is. (throws in an imaginary bucket) *Splosh.* (winds his bucket up making the appropriate creaking noises) I must be careful not to spill any . . . it's very heavy. Here you are horse.

Conversation 4

Colin and Robert building together. (Colin C: Robert R)

1 C: What shall we build first, Robert?

2 R: Why, the shop.

3 C: Yeah—that shop. Let's not build a shop.

4 R: Let's build a tower.

5 C: Yeah. OK. Fetch the big bricks and get those round ones. Let's get one of these, Robert. We need this, we need this.

6 R: We need that pointed thing. I'm getting it. I'm putting the round ones for the gate—like that. I'm putting this one on top—like that. Careful—don't knock it.

Conversation 5

Sandra and Janet playing with the dressing-up box. (Sandra S: Janet J)

1 S: I want that hat. I'm the king.

2 J: It's mine. I had it first.

3 S: You look silly, you're too little . . .

4 J: I'm the king I walk like this.

5 S: I do, too.

6 J: Stop copying me. I'm the king of all of you and no one is allowed to copy me, only Mary, because she's my best friend.

Conversation 6

Peter and his holiday. (Peter P: Teacher T)

1 T: What are you going to do on your holidays?

2 P: We're going to the seaside.

3 T: How will you get there? Will you go by train or . . .

4 P: We're going to go in my daddy's car.

5 T: That sounds exciting. What will happen?

6 P: We'll get up very early and we'll go on the motorway, then we'll stop and have some pop and we won't get there till it's ever so late.

7 T: If you hadn't got a car how else could you go on your holiday?

8 P: Well—you could go on a bus—or a train.

9 T: Any other way?

10 P: Oo—sometimes you can go on an aeroplane. My Granny's going to when she goes to Spain. She could go on a boat but she'll get there a lot quicker in an aeroplane.

Conversation 7

Sally and Kathryn are in the painting corner. (Sally S: Kathryn K)

1 S: Look at that, you've spilt paint all over the floor.

2 K: What will Miss say?

3 S: I don't know.

4 K: Will she be cross?

5 S: I 'spect so, she said to take care.

6 K: Shall I tell her?

7 S: No, she'll be mad.

8 K: I shall have to. What'll she be mad for?

9 S: 'Cos she likes to have the painting corner cleaned by playtime.

10 K: If I say I'm sorry she may not be too cross.

11 S: She'll be all wild and strict, you know. She'll come and shout and I bet she'll make you clean it up when we've all gone.

The reader should now turn to p. 130 in appendix one and compare her judgments with the list provided there.

2 Spot the strategies

Study the examples above again. Can you now identify the strategies used by the child which serve each of the uses illustrated? The reader can refer to the list of uses on p. 80 of chapter eight. While not all the strategies are illustrated in these examples the reader will gain useful practice going through the list and recognizing strategies as they occur in the transcriptions.

An analysis of the transcriptions is given on pages 130 and 131 of appendix one and readers should now compare their own identification of strategies with it.

3 Spot the uses and strategies

The first examples given here have been selected to illustrate different categories, but in normal conversation often there is a frequent change in the purposes for which language is being used. Look at the following two examples. First of all perhaps the main uses of language could be identified and the points at which there is a change from one use to another. Then the reader could go over the examples again and, using the list on p. 80, identify the different strategies that appear.

Conversation 8

After talking about St George, a group of boys were playing with bricks. (Richard R: Simon S: Mark M: Stephen St: Teacher T)

1 R: It's St George's castle.
2 S: It's got flags on it.
3 R: To show everybody it's St George's castle.
4 M: Stephen made this boat, it's guarding the castle.
5 T: Yes.
6 St: Because we don't want the dragon to get in.
7 T: Because you don't want the dragon to get in?
8 St: No.
9 T: I wonder why?
10 St: It will eat all the people. The king and queen and the princess.
11 M: It will knock the castle down.
12 D: It will burn it down with its fire. It will breathe it onto the walls and melt the walls and burn all the wood, 'cos wood burns easily.
13 St: The boat blows a horn and then the men come out. Men come out of the castle over the drawbridge.
14 M: (pointing to the drawbridge) If the dragon is there they come there (pointing to opposite side of castle). They can't get out.

15 T: Yes.
16 M: Because it will breathe fire on them and will eat them up.
17 St: If the horn blows to warn the men that the dragon is coming they get on their horses and gallop away fast as they can over the drawbridge.
18 St: They have to get out because the dragon could knock the castle down.

Conversation 9

Stuart talking about a bus. (Stuart S: Teacher T)

1 T: Now then, what are you going to tell me about this?
2 S: They've all gone in a stupid bus. In a silly old bus.
3 T: Who's gone on a silly old bus?
4 S: The sergeant of all the army.
5 T: And what does he do?
6 S: He calls them to fight and they all went onto the bus 'cos they were scared. And he said 'Come down from there' so they did. He said 'Aren't you going to fight any more?' and they said 'We jolly well aren't'. It's a real silly bus and it's magic and it always does silly things. And it keeps everybody scared.
7 T: And how do you make a real bus go? What's different—what's a real bus like?
8 S: You put your gear in, push your pedal down and then, then fasten your seat belt and go.
9 T: And why do you need a seat belt?
10 S: Because when you have a crash you'll tipple over, and then you won't be fallen out.
11 T: You tipple over if you've got your seat belt on?
12 S: No, if you have a crash and you might tipple over, then you won't fall out.
13 T: What would happen if you didn't have a seat belt on?
14 S: You would fall out if you had a crash. If the door was locked you wouldn't, you would just knock about. The door might flick open.

15 T: Yes, and then . . .

16 S: You'd be dead . . .

17 T: Have you ever been in a hospital?

18 S: Yes, I've been in twice. I had a chin cut open and then a leg. You have a scab on and when your scab falls away you've got a scar.

19 T: It must have been quite a long time to leave a scar like that. Well, what would you like to write on here?

20 S: Here is a very bad bus.

The reader's identification of the uses of language and the strategies employed can now be compared with the analysis given in appendix one pp. 131 and 132.

Applications

Now is the time to put the tape recorder to use and collect examples of children's talk in order to build up a collection to illustrate the uses of language and the strategies which serve them. Transcriptions of short extracts from recorded conversations, like those above, could now be made. If the transcriptions are to be used for discussion, it is helpful to number the utterances for reference. The transcriptions can then be examined and uses of language and strategies can be identified.

Further reading

Several classifications of language uses have been put forward as a means of studying language.

Andrew Wilkinson has summarized a classification of the uses of language suggested by M. A. K. Halliday. This summary can be found in chapter VII, section 3 of Wilkinson's book *The Foundations of Language*. Halliday's classification offers seven models of language use which are illustrated from the language used by his three year old son.

Another view of language use is offered in chapter 2 of M. M. Lewis's *Language and the Child*. Two main functions are described—the manipulative and the declarative—and examples are given to show how these two functions serve a wide range of experiences and behaviour. The chapter includes a discussion of the influence of language on most aspects of the child's development.

The work in which children's use of language in a number of situations is described, is in chapter 6 of Joan Tough's *Focus on Meaning*. The chapter goes on to discuss the factors that can hinder or extend children's learning. These include the expectations that children have when using language with adults, their knowledge of what the adults' expectations will be, the meanings available to the children and the extent to which experiences have offered opportunities for using language.

LEWIS, M. M. (1969) *Language and the Child* NFER

TOUGH, J. (1974) *Focus on Meaning* Allen and Unwin

WILKINSON, A. (1971) *The Foundations of Language* Oxford University Press

Chapter nine

Making an appraisal of the child's use of language

If the classification of uses outlined in the last chapter is to be used by the teacher for making an appraisal of the way in which the child uses language, the uses of language and strategies must become so familiar that they can be recognized and noted during normal discussion. To begin with, observing children in general activities and talking with them about what they are doing, or using the opportunity to encourage them to recall or anticipate relevant and associated experiences, may not be the easiest situation in which to attempt to make such an appraisal. The child's activity may seem to have a wide range of possibilities for promoting his attempts to use language to express different kinds of thinking, but keeping alert to the possibilities which might be pursued, and framing questions and comments that will help the child to give appropriate and thoughtful answers, will at first allow little opportunity for noting the detail of the child's responses. Yet eventually, if an appraisal is to be made of the way in which the child uses language, specific uses must be identified, and some written note made, without any pause in the dialogue between teacher and child. The teacher will need practice and patience to achieve this skill. Once achieved, building up a record and planning future action becomes possible.

Perhaps we should emphasize again that *appraisal* does not mean *measure*. It means *to be aware of* or *recognize the nature of* what the child is doing with language. Making an appraisal means giving an account of what the child shows he can do with language in a particular situation.

The role of the teacher's questions

One important aspect of appraisal is that the child's response may be very much influenced by the kind of question that is asked of him. For example, if questions like 'What's that?' are used, the answers are likely to take the form, 'An apple' or 'It's an apple'. There is no difficulty in identifying this use of language as *labelling*, a means of reporting, and everybody sometimes gives answers of this kind. But when an appraisal is being made if the child is always faced with a closed question—'closed' because it indicates that there are few possible answers—he may never be given an opportunity to deal with 'open' questions, that is, questions to which there is a wide range of possible answers. An 'open' question, for example 'What might be happening here?' or 'What do you think the man might be saying?', allows the child to give an individual interpretation. We should point out, however, that although the kind of question asked might be expected to have some effect on the kind of answer that will follow, some children will give extended responses whatever the question, and others may give limited answers even to open questions.

The teacher will need to use questions that are *enabling* because they seek to help the child extend his answer and reveal his real capabilities The enabling question is one which takes up the child's response and helps him to focus on the basis from which it was made—'Why do you think that?' or 'How did you make that?' If a full view of the child's capabilities in using language is to be gained, then opportunities for using both open and enabling questions need to be recognized and closed questions might be used infrequently, for example only in those situations where the child's attention needs to be directed towards particular features in order to help him take into account all the available evidence on which his response should be based.

Nor should we feel that questions provide the only strategies for stimulating the child's thinking and talking. There is also a need for the teacher to give the child the experience of taking part in a conversation and to do this the teacher must contribute comments as well as questions. Some questions to keep in mind as teachers study their own strategies, and those of others, as they talk with young children, could be: How does the teacher indicate willingness to be an interested audience without asking too many questions? What approaches seem to encourage the child to offer full comments? How can a point of growth for the child be recognized? When should a question be left and forgotten, or answered before passing on to the next? How does the teacher judge when important information should be given, or a summary should be made for the child, or a story line emphasized?

It can be seen that the relationship between the child and the teacher is all-important if the child is to benefit to the utmost from the experience of one-to-one dialogue. The relationship will be different for each child, because of the different combinations of personalities of child and adult. But the engagement should always be, at the least, willingly tolerated by the child, and the teacher must work to make the experience not only enjoyable, but also purposeful.

Talking with a child in an attempt to help him realize his full capabilities of thinking and talking, and so that an appraisal can be made, is clearly a skilled and sensitive task. It should not be expected to come easily; rather it should be seen as requiring experience and a critical examination of the quality of the interaction between child and teacher. Skills of this kind will be considered fully in *Talking and Learning: A Guide to Fostering Communication Skills in Nursery and Infant Schools.*

Using pictures for appraisals

Because making an appraisal of the child's use of language demands concentration and skills which

may take some time and practice to develop, it would seem to be helpful to devise some situation for the first attempts which will reduce the difficulties as far as possible.

Teachers who have developed the skills of making appraisals have found that making a tape recording of a conversation with a child, and then making a transcription of some or all of it, has been particularly useful since they can replay the tape and check whether the attempts at identifying the uses of language during talk with the child were successful. They can also use the recording to examine their own skills of questioning and commenting. If tape recordings are to be made, then the teacher should make use of situations in which the child is likely to remain within range of the microphone. Using a quiet corner in the classroom might be suitable; if it is possible to work outside the classroom, this will further reduce the possibilities of interruption and the interference of other noise. But we would emphasize that we are suggesting that the teacher tries to plan such situations in which successful tape recordings can be made primarily in order to help in establishing the necessary skills for appraisal. The final aim must be to acquire the skill to carry out appraisals in normal classroom situations.

Looking at pictures and books is a common activity in the nursery or infant classroom and it is an experience which is both appropriate and beneficial for the child. Because of this, and for various other reasons discussed below, using pictures or a picture book may be a particularly appropriate situation in which the teacher can begin to acquire the skills of appraisal.

Although pictures may always be interpreted differently by children, on the whole their answers are likely to be within a predictable range. Certainly the questions that are to be asked can be worked out carefully. Since teachers will use the same picture with several children, it is possible for them to study their questions and comments and to improve on these in the light of children's responses. Using picture books, then, seems to be a good way of gaining practice in making appraisals because it is a situation which can remain similar for a number of attempts. Talking with children in other ongoing activities is likely to produce few opportunities for revising the approach from one attempt to another because of the changing nature of the activities themselves. Once the skills of appraisal have been established, however, then almost all activities in the classroom are likely to offer situations in which appraisals can be made.

Another reason for choosing to use picture books for the first attempts at appraisal is that a number of teachers can use the same material and their individual experiences can provide a good basis for discussion. Tape recordings can be compared and each teacher can learn from the others' attempts. Children's responses can be compared and a wider range of uses of language is likely to be produced, so that the opportunities for identifying particular strategies used by children will be increased.

We should point out, perhaps, that not all pictures or illustrated books are suitable for the purposes of appraisal. Many pictures illustrate incidents from a story. If the child has heard the story then this will tend to limit the kind of interpretation he can make for himself. Many pictures which are effective illustrations of a story may not have enough detail in them, or enough action and incident involving people, to give the wide basis the child needs to show the full range of his thinking. Many pictures do not carry through a strong story line and so do not offer the child the evidence from which to make an interpretation that carries forward from one page to the next.

While there are many good picture books on the market, not all of them have pictures which offer a good basis for dialogue. For this reason, we have devised the two sets of pictures to accompany this book. These pictures have the added advantage that they will be available to all the members of a group of teachers, which is not always possible with other picture books. Teachers are asked to note that the pictures are provided to form the basis for a full discussion of their use in making an appraisal. They will be able to have the pictures at hand throughout the discussion and will all be able to use the same book for their work together.

We must also emphasize that the pictures have been provided to help demonstrate a general method of using pictures and books for making an appraisal. Once teachers have worked with these pictures and

mastered the general principles involved, they should then be able to adapt the method to other pictures and books available in their classrooms.

The design of the books

The two sets of pictures *Black kitten gets lost* and *Dad forgets his dinner* have been designed for the specific purpose of helping teachers to make their first appraisals of children's use of language. Since they are rather differently constructed from most pictures that teachers might have used with young children, some time must be spent in explaining the intentions of the complexity, detail and general character of the pictures.

Teachers are asked to remember that it is difficult to construct stories and pictures that will appeal to all children and all teachers. In providing the two contrasting booklets, our intentions are that there will be something in the one or the other that will be familiar to children from both urban and rural areas, that there will be enough of interest within the capabilities of three year olds, and that there will also be enough material in one, at least, to extend the six year old's thinking.

It is important that teachers who use the booklets should not be distracted from examining the principles of making appraisals because the illustrations and stories do not appeal to them. Understanding the principles will help them to gain insight into how to use pictures to obtain a view of the way in which a child uses language.

Black and white line drawings have been used deliberately. Coloured illustrations can often result in additional difficulties for the child, particularly where colours are restricted and not true to life. The line drawings allow considerable detail to be used and to stand out clearly.

In looking at pictures (or indeed at any scene) the child needs to be able to pick out those features which are significant for making an interpretation. Children from homes where pictures and books are an integral part of the way of life are given a long introduction to looking at pictures. The adult who looks at books with the child intuitively helps him to make sense of what he sees, pointing out details he may not have noticed, relating important aspects to one another. The child from such a home does not always look at simple pictures; he will sometimes take more complex pictures from magazines and books to the adult, just to talk about them. It is in situations like this that, even before the child is twelve months old or begins to talk, his experience of interpreting pictures begins. By the age of three, and certainly by five and six, most children have learned how to examine pictures and place an overall interpretation on them. Children who have not met such experiences, however, may be unable to structure or set an interpretation on pictures in this way.

Teachers may feel that some young children will be distracted by the amount of detail in the pictures provided here. But the teacher needs to help children to scan and look for those details which give clues to an overall interpretation. This is an important aspect of the child's skills of interpretation and one which the teacher must encourage and foster. We use pictures a good deal in the nursery and infant school and it is important to recognize that not all children may be able to deal with information given in picture form, or with information contained within the details of a picture. For those children who can scan and interpret the pictures and maintain the story line, the detail offers the opportunity for discussion and the extension of their thinking.

The pictures have been presented separately in order to avoid high cost but each set could be put into book form. Holes can be punched in the pictures so that they can be fastened together with laces and used as books. Teachers may feel, however, that they should make them into stouter books, perhaps mounting the pictures, in order, on both sides of pieces of thin card, and then covering each sheet with clear contact film. Holes can then be punched and the pages can be laced together to make a book using the normal right to left turn of the pages, and the left to right ordering of the story sequence.

Using the picture books

The pictures should not be regarded as a form of test. As long as the pictures provide something of interest for the child to talk about, it does not matter if he is unable to recognize some particular features, or that he arrives at an interpretation which is not the expected one. Any interpretation can be accepted by the teacher before going on to help the child to see what might be a more appropriate interpretation. For example, the child may not recognize that one kitten in the first picture in *Black kitten gets lost* is playing with knitting wool. Any interpretation that the child makes of this incident shows the attempt he is making to understand it and demonstrates how he uses language in his attempts. The pictures offer an opportunity for the teacher to help the child look for other explanations, perhaps those which fit in most appropriately with the rest of the pictures.

Although we have said that the teacher should not view the exercise as one of getting *right* answers, nevertheless there is a problem if the child makes an interpretation of a picture which the teacher knows will not fit in easily with the pictures that are to follow. For example, the child may decide that the first picture in *Dad forgets his dinner* shows a family getting ready for a picnic. This is a perfectly appropriate interpretation, unless it is appreciated that the boy is trying to attract the attention of the man in the street. But the picnic interpretation will not fit in well with the pictures that follow, so it is important that, before leaving the picture, the teacher offers an interpretation which will anticipate the next picture. In *Dad forgets his dinner*, for example, the teacher might say, 'It does look as though they're getting ready for a picnic, but I think perhaps the children's father (dad or daddy, according to which is most likely to be used by the child) has forgotten to take his dinner with him.' Even if the child rejects this and insists on his picnic interpretation, he will have the possibility of a different interpretation to turn to when he looks at the next picture and tries to make sense of it.

Sometimes a child will respond in a way that appears to be very original, and that might be described as divergent, imposing an interpretation which owes more to his imagination than to the cues given in the picture.

In the following example, a child responds to the

first picture in *Black kitten gets lost* with a unique interpretation, 'The mother cat's magic and she's turned the lady to stone so that the kittens can have a good time!'

Although responses of this kind are interesting and can be accepted, we should perhaps help the child to be able to give a more rational interpretation. He should be able to see the limits set on an interpretation by the clues within the picture and to realize that he cannot always profitably ignore these limits or set them aside by some condition of his own, in this case by 'it's magic'.

We would always want to encourage the child to take an original view where this was appropriate, but it does not help him if he begins to feel that any flight of the imagination is always appropriate and that he can make his own conditions for interpretation. He needs help to learn that interpretations should be relevant and possible.

The teacher should not expect to explore all six pictures in the same depth, unless there is plenty of time. On the other hand, there is little opportunity to view the child's ability to use language if none of the pictures are explored in any depth or for as long as the child is interested.

The first picture of each set has been designed to arouse the child's interest in what is happening in the picture and to encourage him to think about what might happen next. So the child should be helped to explore the possibilities of the first picture in some depth because it sets the scene and raises the possibilities of what might happen later. Some children may be content to talk about just one or two pictures and come back to talk about the others some time later. Other children, after having explored one or two pictures in depth, may be impatient to know how the story ends before leaving the teacher. The teacher must judge how the discussion can be quickly brought to a satisfactory conclusion if time is running out.

The purpose of the picture books, then, is to give the teacher an opportunity to talk with the child in a situation in which other distractions will be minimal. The list of uses of language will need to be kept in mind and perhaps at the first attempts it will be useful to have the list on p.80 at hand. The teacher's comments and questions should aim to help the child show the full range of his thinking and the teacher should try to note down the uses she observes.

Eventually, it is expected that teachers will be able to recognize uses and deliberately select a form of question or comment that will help to extend the child's thinking and promote other uses, as well as writing down what is observed. To begin with, however, the teacher may find that it is not possible to make written notes about the child's use of language because of the need to think carefully about the next question. If a tape recorder is used for the first attempts, transcriptions can be made and studied, and the conversation may be heard again and the uses of language observed can be noted down. Teachers working together can listen to the recorded talk and compare their judgments about the uses observed. It would seem advisable at first to concentrate on talking with the child and on trying to recognize uses of language and strategies. We shall consider ways of making written appraisals in the next chapter.

The child's response to the pictures

Each picture in each set provides the possibility for the exploration of a range of ideas. The picture on p. 100 is the first in *Black kitten gets lost*. We can see that it gives an opportunity for the child to give an account, or a report, on what he sees. What details will he notice and refer to? How can we help him to refer to important detail—important, that is, for the interpretation of the whole picture?

The picture offers the opportunity to reason about the lady's concern and to project into her feelings. Why is the lady cross? Why doesn't she like the naughty things the kittens are doing? What is the mother cat thinking? What is little black kitten feeling? What might he think? Where might he go?

The picture allows the exploration of a number of ideas which should give the teacher a view of the range of uses of language available to the child.

But the way in which the teacher approaches talking with the child can hinder or help him in thinking about what is happening.

Here are four examples of teachers using this picture with children. These examples show us the way in which the teacher's comments and questions can promote or restrict the child's use of language.

Example 1

(Teacher T: Mary M)

T: Look at this picture. Can you tell me what this is?
M: A cat.
T: What's this?
M: A plate.
T: And this?
M: A jug.
T: And this?
M: A chair.
T: And this?
M: A tea-pot.

In this example we can see that the teacher's questions place severe limits on the answers that can be given, and leave Mary with no opportunity to do more than name the object to which Miss J is pointing.

This approach is obviously one to be avoided if we intend to help the child show how well he can use language. In this case, however, Miss J (the teacher) is trying to identify the several sounds that Mary is unable to produce, in the way we have suggested in part two. In the case of a young, or very retarded child, it is one way of discovering whether they have learned the names for familiar objects. The alternative technique—'point to the chair'— could be used to find out whether a child can interpret drawings that represent familiar objects. Simpler pictures might perhaps be more suitable for this kind of exploration.

Example 2

(Teacher T: Sam S)

T: Have a look at this picture.
    What can you see?
S: A lady, and a big cat and some little cats.
T: Anything else?
S: They've got some sausages.
T: Yes, they have—what else?
S: Some cups and some chairs and some spoons.

In a way, Sam responds quite appropriately to the question. 'What can you see?' may be interpreted as asking for a kind of inventory. We cannot tell whether this response is governed by the question, or whether this is typical of Sam's view of a picture, whether he tends to see each part in isolation from the rest.

Example 3

(Teacher T: Peter P)

T: What do you think about this picture Peter? Can you tell me what is happening?
P: There's a lady like this (he demonstrates) and that cat's on the table and that one's knocked the tea over. Look at those pulling the sausages and that one's going outside.

Peter here has made a very different reply from that which Sam gives in Example 2. He shows that he recognizes the connections between the objects and people represented. He seems to do more than make a list, but further questioning is needed to see how much of the meaning of the picture he has been able to realize.

Example 4

(Teacher T: Paul P)

T: What do you think about this picture Paul? Tell me what is happening will you?

P: Well—I think the lady's very cross because of all those naughty kittens and she's cross too with the big cat because it's been fast asleep and not stopped them.

T: Why do you say they're naughty?

P: Look what those two kittens are doing on the table—they've made a right mess with the milk and tea. And they might break something.

T: Are the others naughty too? Why?

P: Well—it shouldn't do that to her knitting and they shouldn't have got those sausages.

T: Why do you think the lady's cross with mother cat?

P: She shouldn't have gone to sleep and let them make that mess.

T: Is she really asleep?

P: She might be pretending because they do— sometimes.

Paul's response is different again. He takes in the picture as a whole (he spends longer looking at it, in fact) and then he expresses a meaning for the total situation. He surmises that the lady is cross, perhaps because of her expression, and then he looks at the activities of the cats, perhaps to see why she is cross, and what he sees convinces him that his interpretation is sound.

Paul's first answer gives the teacher an opportunity to ask him to justify what he says and then we see that he is indeed very much aware of the basis from which his conclusion was drawn.

He shows, too, that he is aware that there are sometimes other explanations. He is tentative, using 'might' about the cat sleeping. He also shows that he is able to anticipate possible happenings not illustrated, e.g. 'they might break something'.

Paul is an able five year old and his answers show the complexity of meaning that can be extracted from a picture and expressed through language.

From these examples we can see that each teacher takes a different approach and that each child responds differently.

When looking at the picture on page 100, Sam responds by listing the objects present in the scene, 'A lady and a big cat and some little cats.' Sam seems to monitor his own experience and arrives at a list of items. Apparently he does not reflect upon what he sees, or seek for further meaning by trying to look at the picture as a whole. His response is judged to be *reporting* but only at the level of labelling.

The third example shows that Peter responds to the actions in the picture and organizes the scene into a series of events or incidents. He, too, seems to be scanning the picture, noting a number of separate incidents; again the full meaning of the picture is missed.

Paul's answer, the fourth example, is different from the others: he appears to set a meaning upon the whole scene that takes account of the relation-

ships that exist between the events and the components. He organizes the details so that each adds to the central meaning. Through his language he reveals that the meaning he extracts from the pictures is very different from that of the other children.

It should be remembered, however, that in the examples the teachers asked different questions, and we cannot know whether it was the questions that restricted the answers in the first two examples, or whether the children's responses would have been different if the questions had been more open. If children are to be given the best chance to reveal their skill, then we must take care that the questions we ask promote a full and thoughtful answer.

As the teacher talks with the child about a picture, she will be concerned not only to note the character of the child's initial response but will try to see whether the child can be helped to structure his interpretation more fully through his own efforts. Encouraging noises, 'mm?' 'Anything else?' 'What else do you think is happening?' are the kind of follow-up comments and questions that might help. If the child still fails to see the central meaning he may be helped by having his attention directed to the key figure: 'What do you think this lady is thinking?' 'What do you think she will do?'

Questions of this kind might help to focus the child's thinking, and if the child still needs help the teacher might say, 'I think the lady thinks the kittens are very naughty. Do you?', 'Why do you think they're naughty?', 'What are the kittens doing that's naughty?'

If the child fails to see what is, after all, the central meaning of the picture, the teacher should talk about the kittens' activities, explaining why the lady is so cross, before leaving the picture to go on to the next.

Another important use of language which the teacher will want to stimulate is that of recalling experiences from outside the immediate scene. Almost all the pictures in the two books should provide points of departure from which it seems natural to ask the child to make some associations between something in the picture and something from his experience.

There are scenes in *Dad forgets his dinner*, for example, which are likely to offer links with the child's everyday experiences. The picture on page 163 of a playground comes from this book. All children will have seen swings and a slide, even if they have not actually used them. The picture should provide an opportunity to ask the child questions like the following: 'What do you do when you go to the park (playground)?' 'What do you think the little girl is thinking?' 'What would you do if all the swings were full?' 'What do you think the boy is shouting about?' 'Tell me what you do when you want to go on the slide, will you?'

But we also want to encourage the child to make an interpretation of the picture, so such digressions should not be allowed to distract too much from this. The child's attention can be brought back to the picture by the teacher's comments. How this is done will depend upon the teacher's knowledge of the child.

Some problems in talking with the child

Several problems arise as the teacher talks with the child. It is often difficult to make clear to him the question that is being asked. Questions can be ambiguous and he may not interpret the question in the way expected. The difficulty might arise either because the teacher has not found a way to express the question clearly or because of the child's inability to understand what is being asked.

Sometimes as the teacher talks with the child an opportunity arises for exploring some idea or concept in greater detail or depth. There comes a time when children are interested and able to think about an idea or consider the meaning of a word. For example, in *Black kitten gets lost* the child may be quite happy to consider the difference between a cat and a kitten and to think for a few moments about the meaning of 'young' and 'old'. It is necessary to be sensitive to the child's interest and to abandon such exploration if he is not following and responding readily.

Asking questions itself creates problems. The child is not likely to enjoy the encounter if he feels that he is submitted to a barrage of questions. It is important not to be quizzing him in such a way that he feels threatened. The form of the question should be varied and often a strategy like 'I wonder why' which the child need not necessarily take up, will reduce the feeling that the child is being examined too much. There is, indeed, a need for the teacher to be offering information to the child through comments, as well as extending to the child the opportunity to express his own knowledge. It is also important to note how the child responds when information is offered to him in this way.

One problem often arises when the teacher has asked a question and the child hesitates and does not answer for a while; at this point the teacher is tempted to speak again. Sometimes this happens just when the child has begun to talk and what he says is missed. Often, too, the child is cut short and he does not then have the opportunity to express the idea that was developing. How long should the teacher wait for a child to give an answer? The child needs time to think and it may be that too often the teacher does not wait long enough and speaks just as the child begins to speak. Perhaps restraint from speaking too soon should be exercised, but on the other hand, if there is too long a silence the child may become embarrassed by the attention focussed on him. The teacher needs to develop a sensitivity to the length of time that can pass for particular children before they begin to feel uncomfortable.

On pp. 101 and 103 is a list of examples of different uses of language that have been taken from children's responses to the first picture in each of the books. The examples may help the reader to recognize the different features which are occurring in children's talk. Not all the uses and strategies given on the list in the last chapter are illustrated here.

We will not discuss the use of the pictures further here, but a discussion of the possibilities for their use, and suggestions for the kind of questions and comments that might be used with each picture are provided in appendix two on pp. 146 to 168. This is done so that teachers can study them and become familiar with them, before using the larger pictures with children.

Finally, we would make the point again that the books are not presented as material for testing the child's use of language, but rather as providing a situation which is interesting for the child and offers a good learning experience for him. At the the same time, the books offer the teacher an opportunity to gain a view of the child's skills of thinking and of using language.

Black kitten gets lost   1

Examples from responses to picture 1 of *Black kitten gets lost*

Reporting	*Examples*
1 labelling	'A cat.'
2 describing events	'The cat's jumped up onto the table and is drinking the milk.'
3 sequencing events	'The lady's come in and found the cats on the table.'
4 making comparisons	'That cat's bigger than the others.'
5 recognizing important details or an incident	'The kittens have spilt the milk on the table and one has pinched the sausages.'
6 extracting central meaning	'The lady's very cross about all these naughty kittens.'
7 recall of experience or own knowledge	'My auntie used to have a cat like that—with stripes.' 'We don't give our cat sausages.'

Reasoning	
1 awareness of relationships	'The kittens must have pulled the sausages out of the dish.'
2 justifying judgments	'The mother cat must have been asleep or else she would have stopped them.'
3 recognizing problems	'What will she do? They've spoilt her dinner, haven't they?'
4 reflecting and drawing conclusions	'She is going to have to fetch more milk and more sausages.'

Predicting	
1 anticipating events	'She'll smack all those kittens.'
2 anticipating a sequence of events	'She'll have to clear up the table and make some more dinner.'
3 anticipating problems	'She won't be able to do her knitting now.'
4 recognizing alternatives and possibilities	'She might be pretending (to be asleep) because they do sometimes.'
5 predicting consequences	'The kitten might get lost if he runs away.'

Projecting	
1 projecting into feelings of others	'She's very angry.'
2 projecting into reactions of others	'She'll say "Good gracious me". '

Imagining	
1 developing situation on a reality level	'A boy will find the kitten and take it to school and show it to his teacher and all the children will like it.'
2 developing situation on a fantasy level	'The mother cat's going to do some magic and all the mess will be cleaned up and the lady will be pleased.'

Dad forgets his dinner   1

Examples from responses to picture 1 of *Dad forgets his dinner*

Reporting	*Examples*
1 labelling	'There's a lady and there's a boy and a girl.'
2 describing events	'The boy's waving a bottle and shouting at his dad.'
3 sequencing events	'The girl sees the sandwiches and then she tells her mum about them.'
4 making comparisons	'The man looks littler than the children.'
5 recognizing important details or incidents	'The sandwiches are left on the table.'
6 extracting central meaning	'The dad's gone off without his dinner.'
7 recall of experience	'My aunty lives in a flat and you have to go up in a lift.'
	'My daddy doesn't take sandwiches to work.'

Reasoning	
1 awareness of relationships	'It's a thermos flask to keep the tea hot.'
2 justifying judgments	'The daddy can't hear him because he's so far away.'
3 recognizing problems	'Dad won't have anything to eat for his dinner.'
4 reflecting and drawing conclusions	'They'll have to go quickly to catch their dad.'

Predicting	
1 anticipating events	'Dad will hear the boy banging on the window.'
2 anticipating a sequence of events	'They'll run along the road and find the place where dad works.'
3 anticipating problems	'They'll have to be careful not to get knocked down.'
4 recognizing alternatives and possibilities	'They might throw it down or run after him.'
5 predicting consequences	'If he falls out of the window he'll get hurt.'

Projecting	
1 projecting into feelings of others	'The daddy will be cross when he finds out.'
2 projecting into reactions of others	'She'll say "Oh dear, what shall we do".'

Imagining	
1 developing situation on a reality level	'The children will run away and not come back again.'
2 developing situation on a fantasy level	'The little man's there but you can't see him now because he's invisible.'

Explorations

Using the picture books

1 Using transcriptions

The design of the picture books, the potential they hold for talking with children and the intended method of using them have all been discussed in the last chapter. Two transcriptions are given below to help the reader:

1 consider further the way in which the books can be used to help the teacher gain a view of the child's ability to use language for interpreting the pictures
2 consider how much can be learned about children's skill in using language and about teachers' skills in helping children to reveal their ability in using language through studying transcriptions
3 become familiar with the questions that can be asked about the pictures.

Study the transcriptions of Paul's and Simon's responses and make notes about the uses of language that appear and the strategies that are employed by the children. A list of uses of language and strategies could be written out so that it can be referred to from time to time to keep the possibilities in mind. The uses of language identified can be pencilled in against the child's utterances, together with particular strategies that are identified as shown below. An analysis is given of both transcriptions on pp. 134 to 138 of appendix one.

Transcription 1

Paul (4 years 11 months) looking at *Dad forgets his dinner*. (Teacher T: Paul P)

Picture 1

1 T: Can you tell me what is happening here? Have a good look.
2 P: The boy's putting the coffee down here. The little man's running.
3 T: The little man's running! Um, what do you think has happened?
4 P: Dunno.
5 T: You don't know? What's this? (pointing to food on table)
6 P: Food.
7 T: What is the boy doing?
8 P: He's putting coffee on there and the little man's running.
9 T: I think they are trying to tell dad he has forgotten his lunch. I think they are trying to call him back and say, 'Look, you've forgotten your lunch.'

Picture 2

10 T: Now what are they going to do?
11 P: They've gone out.
12 T: They've gone out, yes. What's happening here?
13 P: They're crossing the road. (pause)
14 T: What is the girl doing?
15 P: She's waiting.
16 T: What else is she doing?
17 P: She's, er, telling the boy they've got to stop.
18 T: Why have they got to stop?
19 P: Because they might push into the car.
20 T: Yes, they might. They are in a hurry, aren't they?

Picture 5

21 T: Now where are they? Have a look at this picture and tell me what you see here.

22 P: Is dad, is dad, half way up there!

23 T: That's him, is it? How do you know?

24 P: I know. (pause)

25 T: You know? What will they do now?

26 P: Get up there and give it to him.

27 T: Get up there? How will they get up there?

28 P: That ladder.

29 T: Well, let's see what happens next, shall we?

Picture 6

30 T: There now, tell me what happens now.

31 P: Dunno, er—little, er—(pause)

32 T: What is the dad doing?

33 P: Erm, erm, putting a pipe in.

34 T: What is that down there? (points to bucket)

35 P: Water.

36 T: It's a bucket of water, isn't it? A bucket on the end of a piece of rope. What has he done with the bucket? (silence)

37 T: He's let it down from the roof. What do you think they will put in the bucket?

38 P: Water.

39 T: Why?

40 P: To make cement.

41 T: What about dad's dinner?

42 P: (pause) I dunno.

43 T: Couldn't they put his dinner in the bucket and pull it up again?

44 P: Yeah.

45 T: Do you think that's what they're doing?

46 P: Yeah! (laughs) He could put his plate up on there. (points to roof)

47 T: Yes, he could. What's dad doing? (pause) He's working on the house, isn't he?

48 P: Yes, mending the roofs.

49 T: Mending the roofs.

50 P: And building a house.

Transcription 2

Simon (5 years 8 months) looking at *Dad forgets his dinner*. (Simon S: Teacher T)

Picture 1

1 T: What do you think has happened here?

2 S: There's daddy and he's got to get his tea down there somehow or other.

3 He was in the building, he walked along there and came out of the building.

4 Mummy said, 'How can we get the flask down to daddy?'

5 T: What might the children do now?

6 S: The children are thinking how to get the parcel of food down to daddy.

7 I think that it's daddy's food for when he's hungry.

8 T: Which room do you think the people are in?

9 S: A building, because it's high from down there.

10 His clothes are being dried and there's lots of things on the table.

11 My house is not a building, it's a house.

12 T: A house is a building. This family lives in an upstairs flat don't they?

Picture 2

13 T: What is happening now?

14 S: They have to cross a road at the crossing so have to wait for the traffic to stop, else it's dangerous.

15 Now it's stopped so they can go across.

16 It's in a town, because it's got lots of shops.

17 That man's going to paint a house so it can be nice—painting the front but wallpapering the inside so any cracks can't show.

18 T: I wonder where the children will go now?

Picture 3

19 S: Now they've come to a park and he said, 'Hurry up or we'll be late there and we'll miss daddy.'

20 She's watching her friend on the swing—she's just stopped swinging.

21 I've never seen a slide like that.

22 I'd go on there for one go and then run to catch daddy.

Picture 4

24 S: Look, daddy's over there on that building.

25 Daddy said, 'I'm up here!'

26 There's a big drip because it was raining at night time, because all of it not got puddles, so it must have been night time.

27 T: What do you think the daddy's job is?

28 S: He's a house builder.

29 T: What do you think the children are saying?

30 S: They are saying they want to go up there with their dad.

31 Daddy said, 'No, you could fall down and hurt yourself.'

32 That's a lorry mixer and he's getting all the sand in the mixer to make a house.

33 They're all going to be for sale. There are lots of doors on the rooms.

34 The daddy will come down that big ladder to get his tea.

Picture 5

35 S: No, they're putting dad's tea in the bucket.

36 They can't go in bucket because they're too heavier.

37 Dad will pull bucket up and get flask and box.

Picture 6

38 T: Now what will the children do?

39 S: Eh, where's the food what was there just now? I was right, they must have took it.

40 Those two must be very hungry now 'cos they've been hurrying.

41 They're going to have some lemonade and an apple and another apple, yes—two apples, and one for the baby. Her got the apples for them. When I runned in I had a drink of tea and some bread with butter on. If we're very good we have bread with some jam on but no butter then.

From the notes made consider the following:

1 Look at the list of uses. Which of these are not stimulated by looking at the pictures? What seems to be the explanation for this?

2 Which uses of language appear most frequently in the responses of the two children?

3 Check your notes with those given against transcription in appendix one, pp. 134 to 138. To what extent do your judgments agree with those given here? Sometimes utterances have characteristics of more than one use of language. The important thing is to recognize why in such cases utterances might be judged differently.

4 Once you have reconsidered your own judgments in the light of those supplied on pages 134 to 138, compare the way in which the two children respond to each picture. Note the differences in the range of strategies used by the two boys.

5 Looking through your notes on the transcriptions, what are the main differences between the responses of the two boys to looking at the book?

2 Finding a central meaning

Many children come into school having had a great deal of experience of looking at pictures and listening to stories. For other children, looking at a picture book will be a new and difficult experience. Particularly difficult for these children will perhaps be the problem of how to extract from the separate incidents in the picture some association, some core of meaning which synthesizes the parts into a meaningful whole. We refer to this as the *central meaning* of the picture.

Looking back over the transcriptions, do Simon and Paul recognize the central meaning of any of the pictures given? How is this indicated and which aspects of the picture seem to have been taken into account by the child in order to make this overall interpretation?

Applications

Further discussion on the use of the picture books is

given in appendix two on pages 146 to 168. Suggestions are made about questions which are likely to help the child reveal different kinds of thinking and using language. Each picture and the questions should be studied carefully so that they may be familiar when talking with the child. It is important to remember that comments are also needed to make the interaction enjoyable so that the child does not feel threatened by too many questions.

Opportunities should now be made to practise using both books with a number of children in order to become familiar with their content and with the problems and possibilities of using them.

Using a tape recorder, so that the conversations can be listened to later, is the best way of recognizing how the teacher's part might be improved. Selecting children of different ages and abilities would give the teacher opportunity to compare the range of responses which might be given to different types of questions and the range of interpretations which children are able to set on the pictures.

Finding other picture books

Once the teacher has become skilled in using picture books in the way suggested in this chapter, it might be fruitful to look for other picture books that could be used in a similar way. What characteristics will these books need to have if they are to be used to gain a picture of the range of language uses which the child employs?

Chapter ten

Making a written appraisal

The picture-story books provide an opportunity to talk with a child and try to stimulate him to use language for particular purposes. At the same time, the experience can be used for making an appraisal of the way in which the child is using language. In this way the books serve two purposes by providing learning experiences for the child and a view of his use of language for his teacher. In the last chapter it was suggested that teachers would first need to try out the suggestions for talking with a child outlined in the picture books, trying to use ways of questioning that would enable the child to reveal his full capability for thinking and responding. Only when the teacher feels able to lead the child's thinking in this way, without having to follow the outline of the method too closely, will it become possible to make written jottings about the child's use of language at the same time. It is essential that the particular uses of language should be identified as they occur: talk flows so quickly that unless we can recognize its character immediately and make a note, much of what the child does will go unrecognized and so may not be remembered.

We have already discussed the principle of *making an appraisal* as meaning the gradual building up of a picture of what the child *can do* with language. By questions and comments we help him to show whether he can use language in certain ways. We aim to give an account of what the child can do in each situation in which we talk with him. Although appraisal necessarily implies making a note of what is observed the teacher will, in time, become so practised in identifying uses of language that it should be possible to make a mental note, when talking to the child, and to make a written statement for a continuing record soon afterwards.

But to begin with, the teacher will need to make written notes while talking with the child, or make the appraisal later by analysing a tape recording of the talk.

Making notes on the child's use of language

It has been suggested that the teacher should become familiar with using the picture books before attempting to make notes. Once familiar with the questions suggested in the books, it will be possible to give more attention to identifying uses and making written notes while talking with the child.

The following points should be made:

1 The first stage in appraising a child's use of language is to listen carefully, making notes in a form that is easy for the individual teacher.
2 The questions asked should aim at helping the child to think and express his thinking in language, so that the teacher might observe the range of his ability in using language.
3 We cannot write everything down, but as some uses are noted the teacher can concentrate on recognizing others and trying to stimulate those not yet noted with her questions and comments.
4 There are many features to note and jotting them down, perhaps in a personal shorthand, will make sure they are not forgotten.
5 Making a written note necessitates identification and therefore perhaps helps us to maintain our objectivity.
6 From the notes a summary can be made of what the child was able to do and also what he

seemed unable to do. For example, his answers to *why* questions might show that he does not yet understand the meaning of *why* and the kind of *causal* answer it requires. This summary would be the *appraisal* of the child's use of language in that particular situation.

7 Considered written appraisals, as described above, can then be added to the continuing record through which a picture of the child's development is being maintained.

8 It is important to maintain a critical watch on our own use of language as we talk with the child. The appraisal we are able to make may be governed by the questions we ask. We must be sure that we help the child to reveal a picture of himself that is not seriously restricted by the questions we put to him.

9 The *continuing record* should perhaps be just a growing accumulation of *evidence* of what the child can do with language at particular points and in particular situations. It should reveal, when read through, the kind of progress that the child is making. An example of a recorded appraisal is given on pages 120 to 121.

10 Appraisals made using picture-story books will provide one view of the child amongst views of his use of language in other situations.

Making an appraisal: an example

The following example illustrates how an appraisal might be made. John is 4 years 2 months and his responses to pictures 1, 2, 5 and 6 in *Black kitten gets lost* are given in full. The notes made by the teacher during the appraisal session, as she talked with John, are given alongside the transcription of their talk.

This teacher has worked out a system of abbreviations to ensure that she can make notes with the least possible effort. The speaker is indicated by positioning quoted speech against a stroke, i.e. teacher's talk/child's talk. In addition, she uses i. for initial, r. for response, and pr. for probe. She uses these to remind her, when writing up her notes, whether the child was able to respond straightaway to her questions and the pictures (i.r.) or whether she had to help the child towards a more appropriate answer by a further question or comment (pr.).

After the transcription of the talk for each picture, some comments are made about John's responses and what seem to be the most important points to note.

John (4 years 2 months)

Picture 1
John opens the book, smiles but says nothing as he looks at the first picture.

T: Have a good look at the picture, John. I wonder what's happening here—what do you think is happening?
1 J: Pussy's wandering.
  T: Yes, he is—what else is happening?
2 J: There's mummy going to feed him.
  T: What do you think the mother will give them to eat?
3 J: The kitten's going outside.
  T: Yes, he is. I wonder why? What is the lady saying do you think?
4 J: She say—go there.
  T: Why do you think the lady looks so cross?

Notes made by the teacher during appraisal session

John S 12.10.71. Black kitten gets lost.
(These notes will later be expanded to form a permanent record of the session.)

interested: pussy's wandering

feed him

art: d/th, d/g, t/k

very short utts. she say—go there

H

John (4 years 2 months)   **Notes made by the teacher during appraisal**

5 J: Kittens do that.

   T: Tell me about the kittens. John talks readily/awareness cause
Whatever are they doing?

6 J: On table—that naughty. pr./that naughty

   T: Why do you say the kittens are naughty?

7 J: Spilled it—spilled it. no detail ref. incidents, no connections

   T: And look at the other kittens—what
are they doing?

8 J: Fighting—fighting for sausages. i.r. no central meaning

   T: Why do they do that?

9 J: They want some. pr./some awareness of causes

    T: They want some to eat do they?
What do you think mother cat is thinking
about her kittens?

10 J: He's going there—out.

   T: Yes he is—do you know why? The lady
is very cross with the kittens because they
have made such a mess—can you see?
They've spilled the milk and spoiled her
knitting. Oh dear. Now she says it's time
they all had new homes. She says she's
going to find a good home for everyone.
So little black kitten thinks he'll set off
and find a good home for himself. Shall
we look and see where he's going? Where
do you think he's going?

Comments on John's talk

First of all we would note that John has some difficulties in producing some sounds. We have not indicated these in the script but it was quite possible to identify the problems during the session. John produces *d* or *v* for *th*, *d* for *g* and *t* for *k*. In spite of this his speech is quite intelligible. The structure of John's speech is immature for a four year old; there are many omissions and failures to make agreement. Many of his utterances are telegraphic in character.

Picture 2

John looks eagerly at this picture and opens up the talk.

11 J: The kitten going faster . . . a doggie i.r./kitten going faster—a doggie running after
running after the kitten. the kitten.

   T: Why is the dog running after the kitten
do you think?

12 J: Because that going that way. (points why?/because that going that way
to kitten running down lane)

   T: What is going to happen do you think?

13 J: He chases him and frightens him . . . /chases—frightens—get runned over
he will get runned over.

T: Why is little kitten frightened?
14 J: Because of the dog.   frightened?/because of the dog
   T: Because the dog's running after him.
      Why do you think little kitten will
      get run over?
15 J: Because there's a load of cars there.   run over?/ because there's a load of cars there
      (points to the road)
   T: What should little kitten do when
      he comes to the road?
16 J: Don't know.
   T: I expect you do really—he must stop—   what should b.k. do?/don't kno
      and look carefully, mustn't he? I wonder
      what will happen—shall we look?

Comments

He has learnt to use the regular past ending 'ed' but has not yet learnt the exceptions: for example,
he uses 'runned' instead of 'ran'. There is little evidence of reasoning although 'because' is used three
times (utterances 12, 14 and 15) for example, 'He will get runned over . . . because there's a load of cars
there.' John uses 'because' but looks only to the pictures for the causes and does not reason about those
possible causes that are not illustrated and that depend on projection beyond the immediate experience—
the picture—for their recognition.

Picture 5

John looks at the picture and begins to talk.

17 J: He's runned over and he's killed.   i.r./he's runned over and he's killed
   T: Do you think so? I think he's all right.
18 J: The man's picked him up.
   T: What do you think the children are saying?   children saying/don't know/
19 J: Don't know.
   T: Well, what would you say if your dad   if dad brought etc /don't know/
      brought a kitten home?
20 J: Don't know.
   T: What else is happening—can you see?
21 J: The baby's in the chair having tea.   pr./baby's in chair having tea
   T: What do you think the kitten is thinking?
22 J: He likes it.   kitten thinking?/he likes it
   T: What does he like do you think?
23 J: Loads of people—children and them.
      (points)
   T: What do you think the mother will say
      about the kitten?
24 J: Don't know. Stroke it—she says stroke it.   Mother saying?/Stroke it—she says—stroke it
   T: The man has brought the little kitten
      to his house. The children are pleased
      to see him.

Comments

Although John talks quite readily and shows interest in the pictures, he responds to isolated items and incidents and does not place an overall meaning on the scene. There is little reference to detail, nor is the central meaning recognized, except in the second picture where the dog is chasing the cat. This picture is simpler than the others, since the central meaning is not dependent upon scanning several incidents, as for example in the first picture, where the woman surveys the scene of destruction. One of John's most complex utterances was used in connection with this picture—(21) 'The baby's in the chair having tea.'

Picture 6

John looks at the picture and smiles.

25	J: He's drinking the milk.	smiles—drinking the milk
	T: Yes, what do you think the little kitten's thinking?	
26	J: He's better.	kitten thinking?/he's better (pleased)
	T: What else is happening in the picture?	
27	J: He's having his dinner.	
	T: Is he? Who is having his dinner?	
28	J: The man and the lady and the baby. (pointing to each in turn)	who?/points, labels,—man, lady, baby
	T: What do you think they're having for dinner? (no response) What do you like to have for dinner? (no response) Would you like to have a kitten?	for dinner?/no r.
29	J: We've got a cat.	you like a kitten?/we've got a cat. pr./no r.
	T: Tell me about him, will you? (no response) What does your cat do—is he naughty? (no response) Tell me about your cat, will you? (no response) What do you think they're having for dinner?	cat do?/no r.
30	J: Don't know.	for dinner?/d. k.
	T: Well—have a look. Is it something hot or something cold?	
31	J: Hot	
	T: How do you know it's hot?	
32	J: All smoke coming out?	why hot?/All smoke coming out
	T: Yes, it's steaming isn't it? It will smell good. What do you like for your dinner?	
33	J: Spaghetti—red spaghetti.	for dinner?/spaghetti—red spaghetti
	T: What do you think the children will do when they've had dinner?	
34	J: They'll play out	ch. do next?/they'll play out
	T: What will black kitten do?	
35	J: He'll go to his mother	do?/he'll go to his mother
	T: Don't you think he'll come to stay with the children? It is a good home for him isn't it? What do you think?	

36 J: He'll stay with them.

   T: What will the children think about that?

37 J: They like him—the kitten. They'll look after him.

stay with them

children think?/they'll look after him.

Lists items, incidents, no detail.

Comments

John's talk is tied very closely to the pictures. He is limited to reporting about the immediate experience. He does not respond to questions which ask him to recall. The only example of anticipating or predicting is utterance 13, 'He will get runned over.'

We can see that John is making an effort to respond to the teacher's questions and comments. He enjoys the experience and is interested in the pictures. John is likely to meet opportunities like this with eagerness: the teacher's probing and the fact that she draws his attention to the important content of the pictures and to the central meaning may help him to begin to look for the important aspects of the experience and to develop new uses for his language.

Making a record of observations

We have discussed earlier in the book some of the problems associated with making a permanent record of what has been observed which can be added to a cumulative record of the child's development. We suggest here two methods which might be useful for recording observations of the way in which a child used language during a short appraisal session.

Both methods rely on the notes that the teacher has jotted down in the course of the session, as she talks with the child. The teacher will have had at hand during the session a list of the uses of language and the particular features to observe, and this will help her to note the different uses as they occur and to frame her questions so as to elicit uses not yet observed; this will help to ensure that the child shows the full range of his ability to use language. The notes the teacher makes as she talks will inevitably be very brief, using abbreviations and probably a form of personal shorthand; they will not be suitable for inclusion in a cumulative record. But, particularly if they are used very shortly after the appraisal session, they do form the indispensable basis for preparing a permanent written record.

Two methods are illustrated below. Method 1 is an expansion of the teacher's first brief notes into a diary-type entry and method 2 is an expansion of the notes into a classification of the uses of language observed.

Method 1

12.10.71 John showed interest in the pictures and talked readily. His speech is quite intelligible although he say *d* fot *th*, *v* for *th* and *t* fot *ck*. Many two- or three-word utterances. Many omissions and agreement errors, e.g. he says, 'that naughty', 'smoke come out'. Doesn't see central meaning of picture 1. After probe says 'kittens do that' so may be some recognition of central meaning. Uses 'because' but does not anticipate possible actions. Finds difficulty in projecting, e.g. What are the children saying? What would you say if your dad brought home a kitten? No response to either. Refers to items and incidents but gives no detail or relationship. Only predictions—'will get runned over'—'they'll look after him'.

Method 2

Name John S *Date* 12.10.71 *Situation:* Looking at *Black kitten gets lost*

Speech

Intelligible, says *d* for *th*, *v* for *th*, *t* for *ck*; omissions—parts of verb, e.g. kitten going faster, a, the, e.g. on table; agreements missed—she say; runned; many two- or three-word utterances; greatest complexity—The baby's in the chair having tea.

Reporting

Lists items, no detail: lists incidents, no relationships, doesn't recognize central meaning in pictures 1, 5 and 6; some awareness after probe. No response to questions requiring recall. Comparison: uses 'faster'

Projecting

Doesn't respond to several questions like 'What is the lady saying?' until picture 5, 'What is mother saying?' 'Stroke it—she says stroke it.'

Anticipating

Only examples, will get runned over, they'll look after him.

Reasoning

Little evidence.

Uses 'because': not cause and effect relationship, e.g. He will get runned over . . . because there's a load of cars on there.

Why is he frightened?—because of the dog.

Why is dog running after kitten?— because that going that way.

One deduction: Is it hot or cold?—hot.

Why do you think it's hot?—all smoke coming out.

The two methods illustrated here may neither of them be the best possible way of recording observations: we are aware that a good deal of experiment is needed in order to discover how much the teacher can profitably note while she is listening to and talking with the child, and whether using a particular kind of layout might help her to record the most important points from the child's talk during the appraisal session.

Whatever method of note-taking is used, it is important that it should not interrupt the flow of the conversation. It is also essential that the notes should be expanded to a fuller comment of some sort as soon as possible after the appraisal session.

If the two picture-story books are used in this way the teacher should find that with perserverance in making written notes, even when this seems time-consuming and awkward, the skill of making appraisals will become well established. It will then be possible to use this skill in other situations, for observing and recording the child's skill in using language.

Explorations

Making a written appraisal

1 Looking at transcriptions

In the preceding chapter, the transcription of a child talking as he looked at *Black kitten gets lost* was accompanied by the teacher's brief notes and by longer comments on the child's ability to use language in a variety of ways. Readers might now like to examine the following transcription, given without any notes or comments alongside. This transcription can be used in the following ways:

1 First read through and note down the main uses of language and then go back over the transcription and try to identify the particular strategies employed by the child.
2 Summarize the points that are important to note about Shane's ability to use language. Write this down in a form which could be added to the cumulative record.
3 Look closely at the teacher's questions to find examples of points where a different question might have helped the child to a fuller answer and a wider range of language use.

Transcription   Shane: Dad forgets his dinner
Picture 1

1 T: Now, have a good look at this. What do you think's happening here?
2 S: He's looking out of the window.
3 T: I wonder why?
4 S: He's holding a flask in his hand. A little girl's talking to his mummy. A mister's waiting outside and that's all I can tell.
5 T: Really! Why is he doing that?
6 S: I don't know.

7 T: Don't you? Why do you think the mummy's looking like that?
8 S: Because she's cross.
9 T: Why do you think she's cross?
10 S: Because the children are carrying on.
11 T: Yes, the children might be carrying on, but shall I tell you what else has happened? This is their daddy—that man down there —and he's forgotten his . . .
12 S: Sandwiches.
13 T: Yes, he's set off to work without them. So what do you think the little boy's doing?
14 S: He's knocking at window to him.
15 T: I wonder why he's doing that?
16 S: Because he wants his dad to see him.
17 T: Yes, what's he shouting, do you think?
18 S: 'You've forgotten your sandwiches. Come back and get them.'
19 T: What's the little girl saying?
20 S: She's saying to her mummy, 'Dad's forgotten his sandwiches. What shall we do?'
21 T: And what's the mummy saying?
22 S: She's cross about it because he's left his sandwiches and she doesn't know what to do.
23 T: Yes, that's it, and what's going to happen next, do you think? What will they have to do now?
24 S: I don't know.
25 T: Really? What will daddy do without his sandwiches?
26 S: He can't have anything to eat can he?
27 T: Well, don't you think they'd better do something about it?
28 S: Why don't they go outside after him? They could run and catch him.

29 T: Yes, well, let's look at the next picture and see what is happening shall we?

Picture 2

 1 S: They've gone somewhere, they've followed their dad.
 2 T: Yes.
 3 S: Where's daddy got to?
 4 T: He's not in that picture, is he?
 5 S: No—all people are looking, they've got his flask and his sandwiches with them.
 6 T: Where have they come to now?
 7 S: They're in the street. They're going across the road.
 8 T: What is the girl saying, do you think?
 9 S: She's trying to stop the boy because the car's coming.
10 T: Yes, and what might happen if she doesn't stop him?
11 S: He might get knocked over.
12 T: Yes, he might do. They'd better be careful. What are they going to do next, do you think?
13 S: They're following their dad.
14 T: To work, do you mean?
15 S: Yes. (Shane tries to turn the page)

Picture 4

 1 S: He's at work.
 2 T: He's at work, is he? What's happening here, do you think?
 3 S: Is that it, is that their dad?
 4 T: You tell me, do you think that's their dad?
 5 S: No.
 6 T: Why not?
 7 S: 'Cos he hasn't got a hat. I think he had a hat on.
 8 T: I think this is his dad, you know.
 9 S: Is it?
10 T: I think so. So . . . what do they want to do with those sandwiches now?
11 S: They're going to take them to him.
12 T: How are they going to get them up there to their dad?
13 S: He'll have to come down, won't he? His

dad might come down. There's a ladder there, he could come down that.
14 T:.   How else could they get the sandwiches to him? Try and think how they would get the sandwiches up.
15 S: I don't know.
16 T: Can you see the bucket there?
17 S: I know, he'll get a piece of string and tie the bucket on and let it go down.
18 T: Why would he do that?
19 S: Well, they could put the sandwiches in it and he could pull it up.
20 T: You've got it right. Shall we look?

Picture 5

 1 S: See, I'm right—they're pulling the bucket up.
 2 T: That's a good thing.
 3 S: Yes, he can have his dinner now and they can go home.

The summary made for the cumulative record on Shane can now be compared with the summary made by Shane's teacher shortly after the session, which is given on page 139 in appendix one.

Applications

Two methods of making written records were suggested in this chapter. The point was made that teachers would need to experiment with both methods to find a format that suited them and included all that it was important to note from each appraisal session. Readers should now try these two methods for themselves, first using tape recordings and transcriptions. The next step is to try to make brief jottings while using the book with the child. With practice, and this is a process of trial and error, teachers should be able to arrive at a method of recording which combines the maximum of important information about each child with the minimum of practical difficulties and does not distract from the child's interest and pleasure in talking with his teacher.

Chapter eleven

Making an appraisal during classroom activities

Once an awareness has been developed of the approaches that help the child to reveal whether he can think in certain ways through the use of the picture-story books, then the teacher may feel able to apply the same method in other situations with children.

The picture-story books are useful in the first place because they provide a subject on which talk with the child can be based. The teacher in this situation does not need to be alert to what might be a suitable topic to introduce. This does not mean that when using the picture-story books there should be no digression from the provided content if the child offers what appears to be an interesting lead, but only that attention may be focussed mainly on using a variety of strategies.

However, although the books offer opportunities for the exploration of different strategies, they are likely to offer a means of stimulating some uses more readily than others. For example, they may offer many opportunities for observing whether the child can project into the feelings of the different characters portrayed, but they may not help the child to show how readily he can build up an imagined scene as he might during self-initiated play.

If the teacher is to build up a full picture of the way in which the child is able to use language, listening to him in a variety of situations is necessary. What may stimulate one child to talk readily and for particular purposes may not be of much interest to another child. Whenever the teacher's attention is focussed in order to observe a child, some impression or information is likely to be gained about him. The wider the range of situations in which the teacher observes the child using language, the more compre-

hensive will be the picture gained of him. Talking with the child during different activities and about a range of interests or topics will build not only a view of his use of language but, more importantly, also give a view of his thinking and feeling. Some situations are likely to be more useful than others for the purpose of making an appraisal, because of the opportunities they may give for helping the child to extend his thinking, and also his play and activity, through his use of language.

It is always easier to make an appraisal when attention can be given to the child for a few minutes without interruption. It will pay, therefore, to plan classroom organization so that children can engage in worthwhile activities without continually needing assistance. This aspect of classroom management is one that needs considerable forethought for it is not just achieved by making materials readily accessible. The teacher must be concerned to build up expectations about choosing activities and pursuing them with interest to achieve a satisfactory outcome. Other helpers in the classroom should also make it possible for both teacher and helpers to have more time for settling down to talk with children.

It would seem likely that different kinds of activity will lend themselves to promoting different uses. Constructional activities, for example, may provide a good starting point for promoting forward planning and predictions or for examining causal relationships. All activities which use material of some kind seem likely to offer opportunities to discuss natural phenomena, for example why a tower of bricks collapses, why watery paint runs down the paper, why some things float and others sink, why some things bend and stretch and others are inflexible. All such activities can also lead to prediction about what is likely to happen in certain conditions.

The most important element will always be the teacher's own awareness of the moment when an approach is likely to be welcomed or at least accepted by the child, and of whether it is likely to lead to a fruitful exchange of ideas.

Many situations then offer opportunities for engaging a child in talk. Perhaps the following are typical:

1   The teacher may recognize a point in the child's imaginative play when talking with him would contribute something new to his play as well as extending his thinking.

2   Anything the child has drawn or painted or constructed can provide a starting point for talking about how it was done, or what lies behind the representation.

3   Interesting objects or living things brought by teacher or child can provide points of interest. The teacher can deliberately invite the child to look and talk, or she can wait for an indication of the child's interest and then proceed.

4   Frequently, the child himself will offer a spontaneous comment which indicates his interest and focus of attention and this can be taken up and used.

5   There are many incidents during the day that are not deliberately planned by the teacher but that nevertheless offer good opportunities for talk: dinnertime, playtime, as the teacher tidies a cupboard or prepares materials. These occasions provide many children with the relaxed atmosphere they need in order to talk freely with the teacher.

6   Clashes of interest between children can become opportunities for talking about their difficulties and for considering solutions to their problems.

What is essential, if the opportunity is to be taken for making some appraisal, is that the teacher should be able to settle down for a few minutes beside the child so that he recognizes that what he is thinking is of interest. If the observations are to be used to add to a continuous record then it will be necessary to make some jotted notes, as we have indicated in the last chapter. Some teachers may feel that making notes interferes with thinking about what to say to the child, and at first that may indeed be true. But unless a note is made, much that is important may be forgotten; and if notes are not made till after the encounter, they may give a more subjective impression than if points had been jotted down at the time. When we rely on intuitive impressions we may also be selecting intuitively and reinforcing the view we already hold of the child. Through deliberate appraisal it seems likely that a more objective and comprehensive view of the child will be gained.

Until the teacher feels confident about making judgments on the spot, a tape recorder will be useful, particularly if it can be used in such a way that the child is not aware of it. Most young children however, will disregard the tape recorder after the first few minutes, on the first few occasions.

If a tape recording is made, on-the-spot judgments can be reconsidered as the teacher listens to the recorded talk. In this way it is possible to build up skill in recognizing uses and in noting down important features of the child's talk. The tape recording also provides the opportunity for considering the teacher's own use of language and for noting what seem to be more and less effective strategies for helping the child to think and attempt to express his ideas through using language, for example:

1   Were there occasions when the child seemed disturbed by being asked many questions?

2   Were there examples of strategies other than questioning?

3   What happened when the teacher followed up her questions too quickly?

4   What happened when the teacher waited longer?

5   Were there examples of restricting questions (i.e. inviting one-word 'right' answers)? Were the responses of all children restricted by them?

6   Were there examples of ambiguous questions which brought confusion to the child?

7   Were there any 'open' questions? How did the child respond to these?

8 Were there any forms of questions which the child seemed unable to meet appropriately?

9 What other aspects of the teacher's behaviour seemed to affect the child's responses?

10 Were any opportunities missed for helping the child to extend his thinking? Could any of these have offered opportunity for (a) helping the child to anticipate, predict, or plan ahead; or (b) project into the feelings of others; or (c) develop the imaginative situation; or (d) give explanations or reason about something within his interest?

As teachers consider their own talk in such situations, it seems likely that they will gain insight into what are the most helpful strategies for helping children to show their capabilities and extend their thinking.

The continuous record

When the teacher feels able to listen with awareness when talking with a child, to recognize particular uses of language in the child's talk and to make quick notes on the spot about what is observed, then making appraisals of children's use of language can become part of normal classroom practice. Appraisals can be made as the teacher is engaged in typical classroom tasks, when talking with the children at the dinner table, supervising milk, moving equipment about the room, as children tidy up, and when talking with children as they follow the activities of the classroom. Any and every situation becomes one in which appraisal can be carried out.

In some situations, however, it will not be possible to make notes at the time of observation; but a mental note can be made even when the teacher is physically completely occupied, and if she keeps a tear-off notepad handy then important points may be noted as soon as she is free.

While it is very important for the teacher to listen to children and try to influence their use of language in every encounter, it is clear that being able to settle down for a few minutes as the child is busy with, or is just finishing some activity, gives

the teacher an opportunity to observe with greater concentration, and also time to develop ideas. But provided some appraisals are regularly undertaken in such conditions—either looking at a book, or when the child is pursuing some creative activity, or making investigations of some kind, or engaged in imaginative play—then other more fleeting appraisals made in chance encounters will help to fill out the picture and perhaps show the child's ability to use language in a wider range of contexts. Keeping continuous records of what the child is seen to do with language in a series of different situations depends upon the teacher developing skills of appraisal and applying them deliberately in any situation.

The continuous record should not be seen as an overwhelming chore. What is written should be brief—no more than is necessary to record anything that has been seen that is new for that child. This continuous appraisal will alert the teacher to children's progress in thinking and using language and in getting on with other people. It will also provide a basis from which the teacher can judge what might be the most appropriate next step for the child to take.

For some children, the continuous record will quickly show that their resources of language are well developed, that they think and use language effectively, that language and thinking have become an integral part of their response to the activities provided in the classroom, and that they have now gained an impetus towards learning that stems from their own desire to know, to find out, and to understand. For these children additions to continuous appraisals might be made less frequently. But it is important that the teacher makes efforts to provide activities and discussion with these children that will challenge their thinking and set them off on explorations of new ideas.

There will be many children, though, for whom the continuous record shows that their resources of language are not fully developed and that talk with the teacher is needed regularly and frequently. The teacher need not jot down what is observed on every occasion that she talks with a child. It may seem suitable, once a picture of a child's capabilities in using language has been gained, to hold in mind the kind of help a child needs and to seek ways of giving him many suitable experiences of talk with the teacher in which ideas are developed. Appraisals may then be carried out at convenient times and suitable intervals, and progress should be seen when the teacher compares one appraisal with the next.

There will be some children who are found through observation to be restricted to a limited range of thinking and of using language. For these children, who need regular daily talk with the teacher, every engagement should be an opportunity to appraise and at the same time promote the child's skills. The two purposes will go hand in hand and the teacher will need to look out for opportunities to help the child to develop skills of language which have not yet been in evidence.

We give below an example of a continuous or cumulative record. Sharon is five and had been in school for about six weeks. Earlier notes showed that Sharon was at first unresponsive to the teacher, giving very short answers, and apparently not wanting to talk with her.

In the notes given here we gain some picture of the progress Sharon is making. The notes will clearly mean more to the teacher than to the reader, but we can see that they are producing a basis from which the teacher can try deliberately, at each encounter, to promote further development.

Notes from Sharon's cumulative record

Date 14.10.75
Situation looking at a picture book.
Still slight problems of articulating, but improving gradually.
Still reluctant to talk.

Reporting
Largely labelling 'cup' 'saucer' 'teapot'.
Great difficulty in sequencing.
Needed help to recognize central meaning. Had difficulty in relating incidents in picture.

Reporting on past experience
I had tea with my Grandma last night—gave some detail.

Predicting
No response to question—What will lady do next?
No response to 'how' questions—How do you get water out of the tap? How do you light the gas?
Looked puzzled—answered 'You do' and listened to explanation.

She enjoyed the few minutes with me, but was keen to 'get through' the book as quickly as possible.

Date 23.10.75
Situation playing with the model village.
Has difficulty still with irregular past tenses—speech clearer, talks more readily.

Reporting
More attention to events: 'The man's walking along the road', 'The lady's going to the shop'.
Is beginning to anticipate questions.

Reporting on past experience
Told me a long story about going to the swimming baths last night with her brother.

Reasoning
Little evidence of reasoning—avoids 'why' questions
Justifying—only example—'I had to wear my water rings 'cos I can't swim yet.'
Responded to 'how' questions after probing—'I rubbed with my towel.'

Enjoyed session on her terms—still avoids questions, but is beginning to take initiative in introducing topics. Anticipates approach now.

Date 30.10.75
Situation talking about her sewing.
Opened up conversation herself—offered information about activity.

Reporting
Able to sequence what she'd done, 'I did the eyes, and then the ears, and then I sewed the hair.'
Offered—'I've seen a clown on telly' had difficulty in giving detail.

Projecting
'It's a clown doll, he's doing funny tricks'—after much encouragement.

Predicting
Planning ahead—'I'll do his arms next, then I'll have to do his legs.' First evidence of anticipating sequence.
She rejected some bits of cloth as unsuitable (too small) but had difficulty explaining why—'I don't want that bit.' Again why—'I don't know.' Nodded at explanation given—'Yes it isn't big enough.'

A greater range of responses appearing and fewer silences and 'don't knows' but only when she is closely involved with subject matter. Is responding much more readily—much progress in last weeks—pleased to talk with me now. Still finds it difficult to leave concrete present.

Date 7.11.75
Situation looking at burnt out fireworks brought by another child.

Enquiring
What are these? Who brought them? Perhaps the first time I've heard her ask a question!

Reporting
She examined them closely, 'It's very black', 'It smells horrid', 'This one's the biggest'. Needed very little help.
Made comparison using colour, size, shape, details. Lively talk.

Reporting on past experience
Very keen to talk about the bonfire she'd been to. In this context—some *reasoning*—'You mustn't go too close', 'My Dad says we can have fireworks next year when I'm bigger' but unable to continue line of thought 'Why are fireworks dangerous?'

I still need to select situations very carefully so that she feels involved. She is beginning to use skills of reporting in other situations, but needs a lot ot encouragement before she will offer possibilities—she likes to be sure of her ground! Has changed much: now offering information readily. Still confused with sequence—but is now recalling and anticipating frequently.

We can see from these notes not only how Sharon is progressing but also the insights that the teacher is gaining into Sharon's problems. We can also see the awareness that the teacher has gained of the skills of using language that can be recognized and promoted. The occasions for appraisal are not the only times the teacher is talking with Sharon. Between these sessions the teacher approaches Sharon and talks with her whenever possible, as she does to all the children in the class. Sharon is one of the children who needs special help from the teacher if she is to come to use language as a means of getting along with others and for benefiting to the full from the many activities that are provided.

Conclusion

Finally, it becomes clear that once the teacher has in mind the uses of language that can be recognized, and has developed the skills of appraisal, then the main purpose of regular talk with the child becomes that of promoting his skills in using language. If we have made our points well throughout the discussions in this guide, then it must be seen that promoting the child's skills in using language is dependent upon giving him new perspectives on his experiences. Promoting the skills of using language will be achieved by using the ongoing activities of the classroom, by using the kind of thinking that they stimulate, and by helping the child to recognize and solve the practical problems that arise from his own activities. Promoting the skills of using language, then, is essentially dependent on stimulating new thinking and new understanding.

Explorations

Making an appraisal during classroom activities

1 Using transcriptions

Once the teacher is familiar with the uses of language and has practised making appraisals of children's language using the picture books, then making appraisals in many other activities should become possible. At first the teacher will need to make a tape recording of talk and make transcriptions of all or part of it. Working from transcriptions gives practice and brings insight into the way in which uses and strategies can be recognized and also into the part the teacher's questions and comments are playing.

Four transcriptions have been provided for practice and discussion. First, identify the uses of language, then the strategies and finally consider the teacher's role. Could it be improved? The transcriptions are from recordings of talk with Paul in four different activities.

Conversation 1   Building with bricks

1 T: Oh! that is a lovely tower. I wonder what anybody who is working in that room can see? (points to a room in the top of the tower)

2 P: They could see, um. mm. mm. . . . They could see about a thousand miles away, a thousand miles.

3 T: What would the school look like, do you think?

4 P: The school would look like a tiny toy.

5 T: A tiny toy. What do you think you'd look like?

6 P: We'd look like—umm—tiny ants!

7 R: Yeah. Tiny, tiny teenies.

Conversation 2   Paul drawing

1 P: Humpty Dumpty sat on a wall. One day he fell into the sea. One day he sat on the back of the wall and he keep falling off, then every day he keeps sitting back on it until he fell off for six hundred days.

2 T: Oh dear, and why did he keep falling off the wall?

3 P: 'Cos he keeps losing his balance. And people haven't to climb on the wall.

4 T: Why not?

5 P: In case they fall into the sea on the other side, and if they fall into the sea they might drown.

6 T: Yes, they might. If the sea were on the other side and they might fall in, then they might drown. And what would they see if they went right down to the bottom of the sea?

7 P: Whales.

8 T: You think they might . . . yes.

9 P: And crabs. And a hippo with a round face and about six or five legs.

10 T: Has a hippopotamus really got five or six legs?

11 P: No, four. No, you know, those things with a round face. What . . .

12 T: Oh, an octopus. What do you think the octopus would do?

13 P: Carry it and get all its legs and use it as a cage.

14 T: Oh, I see, that would be a good idea.

15 P: And it might be friendly and put it up back out of the water and give it a little ride back to the shore.

16 T: That would be very kind, wouldn't it, if the octopus would do that? Could you really have a ride with an octopus, would an octopus really give you a ride?

17 P: If it's friendly.

18 T: Are they really friendly, do you know? Do you know if octopuses are really friendly? If somebody fell in the water, what would you really do to get them out of the water?

19 P: You could swim for them. You could get a boat.

Conversation 3 *Looking at snails on the nature table*

1 P: It's crawling along, it's going slow.

2 T: Can you see the mark it leaves as it goes along?

3 P: It's all slippy, sticky.

4 T: Why do you think it leaves a trail like that?

5 P: So that its mummy can find them if they get lost.

6 T: Well, I don't . . .

7 P: What does it eat?

8 T: What do you think it might eat?

9 P: It might eat grass.

10 T: Yes, it has . . .

11 P: Will it hurt you? Can it bite?

Conversation 4 *Making a jigsaw*

1 P: That's a Chinese monkey.

2 T: Oh, why do you say that?

3 P: 'Cos it's got a tail like gat.

4 T: Oh, I see, all bushy and curly.

5 P: It's a hot country.

6 T: How can you tell?

7 P: 'Cos, 'cos . . . it just is.

8 T: Yes. What can you see that makes us know it's hot?

9 P: There's the sun.

10 T: Yes, and what about those trees?

11 P: They're palm trees, and gat's going to chase gat.

These transcriptions help the teacher to make an appraisal drawn from a number of classroom situations where the opportunities for dialogue are different. Make notes on Paul's use of language in the four situations. From this, write a summary that could be added to a cumulative record. When an appraisal has been made, it should be compared with the record made by Paul's teacher, which is given in the appendix on page 140.

What would you advise the teacher to do in order to extend Paul's use of language and what situations might she use? What would you advise the teacher to do about the way in which she talks with Paul?

2 Using records

By now the teacher will have evolved a method of making appraisals of children's use of language as part of a continuous record.

Using the notes from Sharon's cumulative record on pp. 120 to 121 in chapter eleven the reader should now consider the following questions:

1 What sort of development can be traced, both *within* the uses of language and *between* the uses of language?

2 What seem to be the most important areas in which Sharon needs help? What kind of situations would the reader advise her teacher to provide now?

Teachers often say that they need to know about a child's background. Here is the entry that was made on Joanna's record card when she moved from the reception class at 5 years 8 months.

Record

'Joanna took a long time to settle down when she started school, but is now a happy, easy going child, with lots of friends. She is still a bit shy of some of the bigger boys, but seems to enjoy all the activities in the classroom, although she prefers the quiet, sitting-down activities. Her mother says she never stops talking about school!

Joanna knows the numbers to ten and has made a good start with prereading activities, though she has not yet shown any particular interest in books. I think Joanna will do well in her next year.'

What is the inadequacy of this type of record?

The reader is asked to compare this entry with the notes on Sharon's cumulative record of the development of her capacity to use language, made by her teacher.

The teacher needs information to indicate the kind of help the child needs on entering a new class. How can the cumulative record be used to assist her in this?

Applications

The reader should now start to make appraisals and build up continuing records of the children in her class. Perhaps those showing obvious disadvantage will be the first to be noted. The opportunities for talking with children which arise from all the activities in the classroom should be taken up and those situations which seem to hold the most appeal for individual children particularly noted and used.

Further reading

The reader will by now have become familiar with *Focus on Meaning* but perhaps a further reading of chapters ten and eleven would reinforce the points that have been made in the final chapters of *Listening to Children Talking*.

An account of the research upon which the framework of uses of language is based is given in Joan Tough's book *The Development of Meaning*. The theoretical basis of the classification is explained and the importance of the uses of language for cognitive development is examined.

TOUGH, J. (1974) *Focus on Meaning* Allen and Unwin.

TOUGH, J. (1977) *The Development of Meaning* Allen and Unwin

Postscript

The appraisal of children's use of language is only a first step; it leads us on inevitably to examine the skills involved in fostering the use of language and this we shall do in the book which is to follow, *Talking and Learning: A Guide to Fostering Communication Skills in Nursery and Infant Schools.*

We hope that the discussion in this guide to observation and appraisal will prove to be helpful to teachers whether they are working on their own or with a group. Teachers who follow our suggestions for further reading and making tape recordings and transcriptions of themselves talking with children will, we hope, be amply rewarded for the time they spend on these activities by the new knowledge and understanding they will gain about the role of language in children's learning. We hope also that they will gain a deeper appreciation of their own role as initiators and promotors of the skills of thinking and of using language and, through their interest in what young children can do, that they will renew their commitment to improving the quality of the experiences that are offered to young children in the name of education.

APPENDIX ONE

Using 'Listening to Children Talking'

Listening to Children Talking has been written as a practical guide to the appraisal of children's use of language. It will have failed in its purpose if it does not lead those who read it to develop skills of observing and appraising children's use of language.

Discussion groups and courses are likely to be organized in many areas, using this guide and the set of video tapes, *Listening to Children Talking*, as a basis. Workshop courses are seen as the best way of developing skills of appraisal. The video recordings of teachers and children talking gives an opportunity for teachers to make detailed analyses which are not possible when they are in the classroom. Teachers are recommended to take part in such courses, if they are available, since they provide the best means of developing new skills.

Teachers who cannot take part in a course of this kind may nevertheless wish to follow the recommendations of the guide. They may work alone, or with a colleague, or a number of teachers may wish to work together. We have designed the guide so that it may be useful for the teacher who works alone and those who work in groups.

The guide has been written so that a number of topics emerge, eight in all, as follows:

Chapters 1, 2 and 3	Language and communication
Chapters 4 and 5	The social use of talk
Chapter 6	The quiet child
Chapter 7	Problems of using speech
Chapter 8	The uses of language
Chapter 9	Using a picture book for appraisal
Chapter 10	Making a written appraisal
Chapter 11	Making appraisals during classroom activities

After each of these chapters we have provided materials for thought and discussion and suggestions for practical activities. These will be found in the sections described as *Explorations* and *Applications*. It should be possible for teachers working alone and those who work in groups to read the chapters, follow the transcription and notes provided in *Explorations*, and then try out the activity suggested in *Applications*.

Adequate time should be allowed for reading the chapters that introduce each topic. If teachers are working in a discussion group, the points raised in the relevant chapter could be examined at one meeting and some of the materials provided in *Explorations* could be used. Following this, a week or two could be spent carrying out the suggestions made in *Applications*. These will often take the form of making tape recordings in the classroom, and duplicated transcriptions of short extracts from the recordings, as well as the audio recording, could be brought to the next meeting, and provide materials for discussion for the group.

Some of the activities suggested may lead teachers to ask whether they are making appropriate judgments. We have therefore provided, within the appendix, comments and analyses to which teachers, whether working on their own or in small groups, can turn. These should help teachers to reflect on the basis for their own judgments.

Groups working in this way may want to ask one of their members to act as convener of meetings, so that there may be someone who will anticipate the way in which meetings can be organized and know what materials will be available for discussion.

Information about courses for group leaders, and for teachers who wish to work on their own, can be obtained from the Project Director, Dr Joan Tough, The School of Education, The University, Leeds. The video tapes, a booklet on organizing courses based on this material, and worksheets for course members, can be obtained from Drake Educational Associates.

Explorations

The uses of language

1 Spot the uses

The main uses of language in each of the conversations given in chapter eight pages 87 to 88 are as follows:

1 Towards logical reasoning
2 Reporting
3 Imagining
4 Directing
5 Self-maintaining
6 Predicting
7 Projecting

2 Spot the strategies

The strategies used in conversations 1 to 7 on pages 87 to 88 are given below.

Conversation 1

Jason on the climbing frame.

Use of language

Towards logical reasoning.

Strategies

1 Justifying judgments and actions.
  Recognizing causal and dependent relationships.
  Recognizing a principle.
3 Recognizing causal and dependent relationships.
5 Reflecting on events and drawing conclusions, recognizing principle.

Conversation 2

Wanda talking about pets on the farm.

Use of language

Reporting on recalled experience.

Strategies

1 Labelling. Referring to detail. Referring to incidents, making comparison.
3 Recognizing related aspects.
  Referring to the sequence of events.
5 Labelling. Referring to detail. Referring to incidents.
  Reflecting on experience and own feelings.

Conversation 3

Andrew and his horse.

Use of language

Imagining.

Strategies

1 Building up imagined role.
3 Recognizing related aspects in a question.
5 Imagining reactions of others.
7 Monitoring own actions. Reflecting on the meaning of experiences.

Conversation 4

Colin and Robert building together.

Use of language

Directing.

Strategies

1 Anticipating possible actions.
3 Considering action.
4 Anticipating collaboration.
5 Directing actions of others and self.
6 Collaborating, monitoring own actions, focussing control.

Conversation 5

Sandra and Janet playing with the dressing-up box.

Use of language

Self-maintaining.

Strategies

1 Referring to physical needs, attention to self.
2 Justifying claims.
3 Criticising others.
4 Justifying behaviour.
5 Protection of self interest.
6 Protection of self and self interest. Justifying behaviour and claims.

Conversation 6

Peter and his holiday.

Use of language

Predicting.

Strategies

2 Anticipating events.

4 Predicting—relevant detail
6 Anticipating a series of events. Predicting outcome.
8 Anticipating and recognizing alternative courses of action.
10 Anticipating the detail of actions or events. Recognizing alternative possibilities.

Conversation 7

Sally and Kathryn in the painting corner.

Use of language

Projecting.

Strategies

1 Labelling the components of the scene.
2 Projecting into the reactions of others.
4 Projecting into the feelings of others.
5 Projecting into other's view.
6 Question seeking direction of actions.
7 Projecting into feeling of others.
8 Anticipating actions of self.
   Question projecting into causes.
9 Projecting into the reactions of others, aware of related aspects.
10 Projecting into the feelings of others, and anticipating reaction to self.
11 Projecting into the feelings of others.
   Projecting into the reactions of others, anticipating sequence of events.

3 Spot the uses and strategies

Conversation 8

Transcription with main uses, strategies, and changes from one use to another, indicated. The whole of the following conversation is in an imaginary and largely fantasy situation. (Richard R: Simon S: Mark M: Teacher T: Stephen St)

1 R: It's St George's castle.	*Reporting present* extracting central meaning
2 S: It's got flags on it.	*Reporting* referring to detail
3 R: To show everybody it's St George's castle.	*Towards logical reasoning* justifying action
4 M: Stephen made this boat, it's guarding the castle.	*Reporting* referring to incident
5 T: Yes.	
6 St: Because we don't want the dragon to get in.	*Towards logical reasoning* justification based on reflecting on own feelings
7 T: Because you don't want the dragon to get in?	
8 St: No.	
9 T: I wonder why?	
10 St: It will eat all the people. The king and queen and the princess.	*Predicting* anticipating detail of events
11 M: It will knock the castle down.	*Predicting* anticipating event
12 D: It will burn it down with its fire. It will breathe it on the walls and melt the walls and burn all the wood 'cos wood burns easily.	*Predicting* anticipating action and events and consequence of actions and events *Towards logical reasoning* recognizing principle
13 St: The boat blows a horn and then the men come out. Men come out of the castle over the drawbridge.	*Predicting* predicting the con equence of action
14 M: If the dragon is there, they come there. They can't get out.	*Towards logical reasoning* recognizing causal dependent relationships
15 T: Yes	
16 M: Because it will breathe fire on them and eat them up	*Towards logical reasoning* justifying action (they come there)
17 St: If the horn blows to warn the men that the dragon is coming they get on their horses and gallop away as fast as they can over the drawbridge.	*Predicting* predicting the consequences of actions or events
18 St: They have to get out because the dragon could knock the castle down.	*Predicting* anticipating a problem and possible solution

Conversation 9
(Teacher T: Stuart S)

1 T: Now then, what are you going to tell me about this?	
2 S: They've all gone in a stupid bus. In a silly old bus.	*Reporting* referring to detail
3 T: Who's gone on a silly old bus?	

4 S: The sergeant of all the army.	*Reporting* referring to detail
5 T: And what does he do?	
6 S: He calls them to fight and they all went onto the bus 'cos they were scared. And he said 'Come down from there' so they did. He said 'Aren't you going to fight any more?' and they said 'We jolly well aren't.' It's a real silly bus and it's magic and it always does silly things. And it keeps everybody scared.	*Reporting* referring to incidents sequence of events detail
7 T: And how do you make a real bus go? What's different—what's a real bus like?	
8 S: You put your gear in, push your pedal down and then, then fasten your seat belt and go.	*Reporting* sequence of actions
9 T: And why do you need a seat belt?	
10 S: Because when you have a crash you'll tipple over, and then you won't be fallen out.	*Towards logical reasoning* recognizing problem and solution
11 T: You tipple over if you've got your seat belt on?	
12 S: No, if you have a crash and you might tipple over, then you won't fall out.	*Towards logical reasoning* recognizing causal and dependent relationships
13 T: What would happen if you didn't have a seat belt on?	
14 S: You would fall out if you had a crash. If the door was locked you wouldn't, you would just knock about. The door might flick open.	*Predicting* anticipating problems and possible solutions predicting consequence of events
15 T: Yes, and then	
16 S: You'd be dead . . .	*Predicting* anticipating event
17 T: Have you ever been in a hospital?	
18 S: Yes, I've been in twice. I had a chin cut open and then a leg. You have a scab on and when your scab falls away you've got a scar.	*Reporting* (past) referring to sequence of events and detail
19 T: It must have been quite a long time to leave a scar like that. Well, what would you like to write on here?	
20 S: Here is a very bad bus.	*Reporting* making a judgment

Explorations

Using the picture books

Transcription 1 Paul looking at 'Dad forgets his dinner'

Picture 1

(Teacher T: Paul P)

1 T: Can you tell me what is happening here?
Have a good look.

2 P: The boy's putting the coffee down here.
The little man's running.

Reporting referring to incidents and labelling actions

3 T: The little man's running! Um, what do you think has happened?

4 P: Dunno.

5 T: You don't know? What's this?
(pointing to food on table)

6 P: Food.

Reporting labelling (limited by question)

7 T: What is the boy doing?

8 P: He's putting coffee on there and the little man's running.

Reporting affirming first response

9 T: I think they are trying to tell dad he has forgotten his lunch. I think they are trying to call him back and say, 'Look, you've forgotten your lunch.'

Picture 2

10 T: Now what are they going to do?

11 P: They've gone out.

Reporting labelling action

12 T: They've gone out, yes.
What's happening here?

13 P: They're crossing the road. (pause)

Reporting labelling action

14 T: What is the girl doing?

15 P: She's waiting.

Reporting labelling action

16 T: What else is she doing?

17 P: She's, er, telling the boy they've got to stop.

Projecting into the reactions and intentions of others

18 T: Why have they got to stop?

19 P: Because they might push into the car.

Predicting possible consequences of actions

20 T: Yes, they might. They are in a hurry,
        aren't they?

Picture 5

21 T: Now where are they? Have a look at
        this picture and tell me what you see here.
22 P: Is dad, is dad, half way up there!   *Reporting* reference to detail
23 T: That's him, is it? How do you know?
24 P: I know. (pause)
25 T: You know? What will they do now?
26 P: Get up there and give it to him.   *Predicting* anticipating action
27 T: Get up there? How will they get up there?
28 P: That ladder.   *Prediction* labelling—(implied solution)
29 T: Well, let's see what happens next, shall we?

Picture 6

30 T: There now, tell me what happens now.
31 P: Dunno, er—little, er—(pause)
32 T: What is the dad doing?
33 P: Erm, erm, putting a pipe in.   *Reporting* labelling action
34 T: What is that down there? (points to bucket)
35 P: Water.   *Reporting* labelling (limiting question)
36 T: It's a bucket of water, is it? A bucket
        on the end of a piece of rope. What
        has he done with the bucket? (silence)
37 T: He's let it down from the roof. What
        do you think they will put in the bucket?
38 P: Water.   *Predicting* labelling
39 T: Why?
40 P: To make cement.   *Predicting* anticipating action and intentions

41 T: What about dad's dinner?
42 P: (pause) I dunno.
43 T: Couldn't they put his dinner in the
        bucket and pull it up again?
44 P: Yeah.
45 T: Do you think that's what they're doing?
46 P: Yeah! (Laughs) He could put his plate   *Predicting* possibility for action
        up on there. (points to roof)
47 T: Yes, he could. What's dad doing?
        (pause) He's working on the house, isn't he?
48 P: Yes, mending the roofs.   *Reporting* reference to actions
49 T: Mending the roofs.
50 P: And building a house.   *Reporting* reference to actions

Transcription 2   Simon looking at 'Dad forgets his dinner'

Picture 1

(Teacher T: Simon S)

1 T:	What do you think has happened here?	
2 S:	There's daddy and he's got to get his tea down there somehow or other.	*Projecting* recognition of problem
3	He was in the building, he walked along there and came out of the building.	*Projecting* into situation
4	Mummy said 'How can we get the flask down to daddy?'	*Projecting* into reaction of others
5 T:	What might the children do now?	
6 S:	The children are thinking how to get the parcel of food down to daddy.	*Projecting* into reaction of others
7	I think that it's daddy's food for when he's hungry.	*Projecting* into possibilities of situation
8 T:	Which room do you think the people are in?	
9 S:	A building, because it's high from down there.	*Towards logical reasoning* recognizing a principle
10	His clothes are being dried and there's lots of things on the table.	*Reporting* referring to detail
11	My house is not a building, it's a house.	*Reporting* implied comparison
12 T:	A house is a building. This family live in an upstairs flat.	

Picture 2

13 T:	What is happening now?	
14 S:	They have to cross a road at the crossing so they have to wait for the traffic to stop, else it's dangerous.	*Projection* into possibilities of situation
15	Now it's stopped so they can go across.	*Reporting* recognition of sequence and dependent relationship
16	It's in a town because it's got lots of shops.	*Logical reasoning* recognition of general principle
17	That man's going to paint a house, so it can be nice—painting the front but wall-papering the inside so any cracks can't show.	*Projection* into others' reactions and intentions
18 T:	I wonder where the children will go now?	

Picture 3

19 S:	Now they've come to a park and he said, 'Hurry up or we'll be late there and we'll miss daddy.'	*Projecting* recognizing the central meaning Projecting into the reaction of others

20	She's watching her friend on the swing— she's just stopped swinging.	*Reporting* reference to actions
21 T:	I've never seen a slide like that.	*Reporting* recalled experience
22 S:	I'd go on there for one go and then run to catch daddy.	*Reporting* reflecting on own feelings and reactions
23 T:	I wonder how much further the children must go before they find their dad?	

Picture 4

24 S:	Look, daddy's over there on that building.	*Reporting* detail (location)
25	Daddy said, 'I'm up here!'	*Projecting* into the reactions of others
26	There's a big drip because it was raining at night time, because all of it not got puddles, so it must have been night time.	*Logical reasoning* looking for an explanation of conditions
27 T:	What do you think daddy's job is?	
28 S:	He's a house builder.	*Reporting* recognizing implied meaning
29 T:	What do you think the children are saying?	
30 S:	They are saying they want to go up there with their dad.	*Projecting* into reactions of others
31	Daddy said, 'No, you could fall down and hurt yourself.'	*Projecting* into reactions of others
32	That's a lorry mixer and he's getting all the sand in the mixer to make a house They're all going to be for sale.	*Projection* recognizing intention of others
33	There are lots of doors on the rooms.	*Reporting* detail
34	The daddy will come down that big ladder to get his tea.	*Projection* into reaction of others

Picture 5

35 S:	No, they're putting daddy's tea in the bucket.	*Reporting* referring to incidents
36	They can't get in bucket because they too heavier.	*Towards logical reasoning* recognizing causal and dependent relationships
37	Dad will pull bucket up and get flask and box.	*Projection* into intentions of others

Picture 6

38 T:	Now what will the children do?	
39 S:	Eh, where's the food that was there just now? I was right, they must have took it.	*Reporting* confirming prediction

40 Those two must be very hungry now
'cos they've been hurrying.

Projecting into the feelings of others and *reasoning* about possibilities

41 They're going to have some lemonade
and an apple and another apple, yes—
two apples and one for the baby. Her got
the apples for them. When I runned
in I had a drink of tea and
some bread with butter on. If
we're very good we have bread
with some jam on but no
butter then.

Projecting into implications of scene. Reference to detail. Recognizing related aspects

Reporting on past experience.
Referring to detail and incident.

Towards logical reasoning recognizing dependent relationship

Explorations

Making a written appraisal

Shane: a cumulative record from page 115

Dad forgets his dinner 20.11.75

Reporting	*Central meaning* on most pictures, 2, 4, 5 and looking for interpretation on others; actions of people as well as things—'People are looking', 'A little girl's talking to his mummy'. Sees detail—'they've got his flask and his sandwiches'. Asks *questions* when needs information.
Reasoning	*Cause and effect*—' 'cos the children are carrying on', 'because the car is coming', ' 'cos he hasn't got a hat'. Finds *solutions*—'come down ladder'. But avoids some why questions.
Predicting	Sees *problem* easily—'he can't have anything to eat', 'he'll have to come down'. Predicts *actions*—'They could run and catch him'. Sees *consequences*—'He might get knocked over'. *Sequencing* more difficult; one example—string-bucket-sandwiches.
Projecting	very easily: feelings and reactions—'because she's cross', ' "My dad's forgot his lunch" ', 'She's trying to stop the boy'.

Explorations

Making an appraisal during classroom activities

A cumulative record made by Paul's teacher

Date 12.5.75 *Building with bricks, with Robert*

Engrossed in building; not very willing to talk at first, a little hesitation.

Projecting: 'they could see . . . 1,000 miles'—experiences of others.

Predicting: 'school . . . tiny toy . . . we'd look like tiny ants'—good anticipation of detail.

Willing and able to take up invitation to make comparison, but anxious to continue play with Robert. Perhaps questions should have taken this into account.

Date 14.5.75 *Talking about drawing*

Reporting: In an imagined fantasy situation. Gave detail—'into the sea', 'on the back of the wall', 'six hundred days', 'hippo with a round face', 'six or five legs'. Sequence not clear at first but good later: 'other side', 'fall in . . . drown', 'octopus friendly . . . out of water . . . ride back to shore'.

Predicting: the consequences of actions, 'if they fall into sea they might drown', 'it might be friendly and give it a little ride'; anticipating detail, 'carry it and get all its legs and use it as a cage'. Alternatives: 'you could swim . . . get a boat'.

Reasoning: ''cos he keeps losing his balance'—causal relationship; justification—'in case they fall', 'if it's friendly' (octopus).

Paul was much happier talking about his picture (he still seems to see this as the appropriate time to talk to the teacher, based on expectation of previous teacher to 'do a drawing and write a story') and he projects in a fantasy situation easily. Does he think an octopus can be friendly? He seems to confuse reality and fantasy. Missed agreement of verb and participle—'he keep falling'.

Date 16.5.75 *Looking at snails on the nature table*

Reporting on detail—crawling/going slow.

Reasoning: offered a reason why the snail left a trail, although it shows confusion of own feelings with snail's.

Predicting: might eat grass (after prompt).

Asked three questions seeking information about the snails. Very excited looking at the snails, welcomed my presence to offer information about them. Paul brings his attention to detail to the close observation of natural phenomena, he needs help in making sense of all this information he is taking in.

Date 20.5.75 *Making a jigsaw*

Reporting: labelling—'Chinese monkey', 'palm trees', 'the sun', 'it's a hot country'—central meaning.

Predicting: quite spontaneously—'that's going to chase that' (pointing to a lion and zebra).

Spontaneous offering of information about the picture, central meaning and projecting into action of animals. Paul clearly appreciates meaning but needs help to become explicit, relies on gesture, pointing and use of pronouns, e.g. 'tail like that', 'that will chase that'. Alert to intentions and implications of picture but needs help in expressing his understanding. Not always aware of reasons for judgment, e.g. could not explain why he knew it was hot, although perhaps he knew that lions live in hot countries. Has some problems of articulation—substitutes *g* for *th* in some words. Must try to help clear this up.

APPENDIX TWO

144

Using the picture books

Two sets of pictures accompany this book. Suggestions for putting the sets of pictures together to make the picture books have already been described on page 94. Ways of using these two picture books, *Black kitten gets lost* and *Dad forgets his dinner* have also been discussed on pages 94 to 99. The pictures are reproduced here for two different purposes. First, they are included in order to give the teacher an opportunity to study them and consider possible approaches for helping the child to examine and interpret the pictures without using the full-size picture books. Under each picture there are suggestions about the questions that might be asked in order to help the child demonstrate the range of uses of language that he can employ. Reading these through before using the picture books with children can alert the teacher to the best ways of approaching the child.

Secondly, it may also be helpful for the teacher to have these smaller pictures and comments open as the child is looking at the larger pictures. From time to time the teacher may then refer to the suggestions.

We have already discussed the use of the picture books, but it may be a useful reminder to summarize the points again here. The picture books have been designed with two aims in mind. The first aim, as we have already said, is to provide a situation in which the child will be helped to reveal the skill he has in using language so that the teacher may make an appraisal of it.

Looking at a picture book and talking about it is an activity with which many children are familiar and which they have learned to enjoy. Looking at this book will provide an opportunity for them to show what they have already learned about setting interpretations upon the pictures they look at.

Some children, however, have had little experience of looking at picture books and the second aim of the books is to provide an opportunity for these children to learn how to interpret pictures and to recognize the sequence of a story. The picture books should provide essential experience which some children may have missed.

The two aims, however, need not be pursued separately. We hope that in using the books for the purpose of appraising the child's skill in using language, the teacher will at the same time be helping the child to find the central meaning of each picture and to select the features that link one picture with the next and provide a story line.

Each picture has been provided with a setting and content which should be sufficiently interesting to the child to form a basis for considerable talking. From the child's initial response the teacher will be able to decide whether the best use of the book for that particular child will be to explore each picture in some detail and depth and return to it on several occasions, or whether it is possible to spend enough time on this one occasion to explore all the pictures in some depth. If, from the start, the child is impatient and anticipating the next part of the story, showing his inability to examine the picture in detail even with the help of the teacher, then it may be better to concentrate on helping the child to discover the central meaning of each picture and find the links between one picture and the next. Further explorations of the pictures can be left for other occasions when the child may be helped to consider the details of the picture more extensively.

There is a discussion of the ways in which the picture-story books might be used on pages 94 to 99 and a discussion of the features to be observed and encouraged when talking with children on pages 97 to 98.

In order to guide the teacher during the first occasions on which each picture-story book is used, some suggestions for promoting discussion with the child are given in the following pages. We would emphasize that the suggested approaches should not be regarded as prescriptive. The child's initiatives and responses should be accepted and if possible used to develop the discussion. So in talking with the child about the pictures the teacher is looking for ways of responding to the child so that he is encouraged to think about aspects of the pictures or related incidents.

Observing the child's use of language

A recorded example of a child looking at *Black kitten gets lost* is given in chapter ten, pages 109 to 113. Comments on this child's language are given on the same pages, and suggested methods for noting down observations are given on pages 113 and 114. An example of abbreviations used for note-taking is discussed.

None of the methods of recording comments suggested in chapter ten should be taken as prescriptive. More satisfactory methods can be worked out to suit particular teachers.

It is important that the teacher uses comments as well as questions. Some children will not give appropriate answers to questions and will seem to have difficulty in interpreting the pictures. The teacher should then point out the important features from which the central meaning is constructed and state the central meaning before moving to the next picture.

Black kitten gets lost

Picture 1

Central meaning

The child should be helped to establish a central meaning containing the following ideas:

The lady is upset or cross because the kittens are being naughty.

Opening questions

The first comment or question should be in the form of an open invitation to the child to make what he can of the scene.

What do you think is happening here?
Whatever is the matter here?
Tell me about this picture will you?

Follow-up questions and comments

If the child shows he is not aware of the central meaning and starts by listing items or incidents, then the teacher might help the child to see the connection between the lady and the kittens by asking:

Why is the lady so upset?
What are the kittens doing?
Do you think the lady's cross? Why is she cross?

Reasoning

The child might respond to the first question by giving a full interpretation that shows he has extracted the central meaning and relevant dimensions for his interpretation. If the child indicates that he is aware of the central meaning but does not give explanations then more questions should ask him to offer reasons for what he has said, e.g.:

Why do you think that?

Why? What are the kittens doing?

Discussion can centre then on the antics of the kittens.

As the child finds reasons for the lady being cross the teacher can give supportive comments. For example, if the child says 'Because it's spoiling her knitting', the teacher might say *'What will the lady do now?'* Or if the child says, 'They're fighting about the sausages', the teacher might say *'They are fighting about the sausages. I wonder why?'* The child might be helped to show whether he can reason further, e.g. 'She'll have to start again' or 'Because they're very hungry'.

Projecting

One of the most important observations to make is whether the child is able to project into other people's thinking. The child can be asked to project into what the various characters are thinking or saying:

I wonder what the lady's saying.
What do you think the mother cat's thinking?
What do you think black kitten is going to do?

Associated discussion

With some children the teacher might discuss their own pets or school pets and incidents that have happened at home.

Predicting

The teacher can see whether the child is able to predict:

What will the lady do now?
What will happen to the sausages?

Link with next picture

I wonder what that little black kitten is going to do?

Black kitten gets lost   1

Picture 2

Central meaning

This would contain the following ideas:

A big dog is chasing little black kitten towards a busy road and if he runs onto the road, he might get hurt.

Opening questions

Tell me about this picture.
What is happening here?
Whatever is happening to little black kitten now?

If the child does not seem to be aware of the central meaning, the next question should help the child to link the dog and the kitten and the danger ahead, e.g.:

Why is little black kitten running so fast?
Do you think black kitten is running away from the dog? Why is he running away?
What kind of road are they coming to?

Follow-up questions and comments

Reasoning

If or when the child indicates that he is aware of the central meaning, then he can be asked to elaborate on the basis of his judgments about the picture, so that he can show whether he is aware of the implications of his judgments.

Why do you think the dog is chasing the kitten?
Is this a busy road? Why do you say it's busy?

Projecting

What might the big dog be thinking?
What might black kitten be thinking?
Do you think the kitten might be frightened? Why?
What is black kitten going to do?
What is the dog going to do?

Associated discussion

The child might want to talk about the lorries and vans, where they are going and what they are carrying:

What are the lorries carrying? How can we tell?
He might recall his own experiences of travelling by car or bus. Or the child might recall his own experiences of traffic and busy roads, and the kinds of things that happen on busy roads.

Link with next picture

The link with the next picture should help the child to see the range of possible happenings and help to suggest ways of avoiding accidents:

What do you think will happen to black kitten now?
What is going to happen next do you think? What should black kitten do now?
What do you think the dog should do now? Do you think he will? Why? or Why not?

Black kitten gets lost 2

Picture 3

Central meaning

This would contain the following ideas:
The kitten has reached the main road safely, but he might be in danger from the traffic.

Opening questions

What is happening here, do you think?
What is black kitten doing now?

Follow-up questions

1   If the child does not indicate awareness of the central meaning, the teacher might ask:
Where is black kitten now?
How do you know the road is a busy one?
What will happen if the black kitten goes on running?
2   If the child shows awareness of the central meaning, then the teacher might take the opportunity to help the child reason further about the picture.

Reasoning

Why would black kitten want to get on the bus?

Why do people go on buses?
Can people travel by any other means?

Projecting

What do you think the boy in the bus is thinking?
What do you think the man in the lorry is thinking?
What is black kitten thinking? What does he want to do?

Predicting

What will black kitten do now?
What should you do when you're near a busy road?
What's the best way to cross a busy road?

Associated discussion

The child might recall his own experience of going on a bus.
What are bridges for?
What might go over this bridge?

Link with next picture

Will anyone stop to look after black kitten?
I wonder what will happen to him?

Black kitten gets lost 3

Picture 4

Central meaning

This contains the following ideas:
The window cleaner has stopped his van to see what has happened to little black kitten and to take care of him because little black kitten is lost.

Opening questions

Now, what do you think is happening here?
What is happening to little black kitten now?

Follow-up questions

1 If the child does not see that the man has stopped to look after black kitten, the teacher might say:
Why has the man got out of his van?
What is the man going to do?
Is the man going to pick black kitten up? Why?
Is it a good thing that the man has stopped? Why?
2 If the child shows awareness of the central meaning, then the reasons for his statements can be explored, and the other details of the picture can be discussed.

Reasoning

Why do you think the man stopped?
What kind of job does the man do? How do you know?
How do you know the man is a window cleaner?
What kind of job must he do with a bucket and a ladder and a cloth?

Projecting

The picture gives a good opportunity to see whether the child is able to project into the thoughts and feelings of both the man and black kitten:
What do you think the man is thinking?
What do you think the man is saying to black kitten?
What is black kitten thinking?
What would he like to say to the man?
What does black kitten want the man to do?

Predicting

There is also an opportunity here to see whether the child is able to predict a likely outcome to the situation:
What do you think the man will do now?
Where will the man go now?
What do you think black kitten will do now?

Associated discussion

The teacher might ask the child to talk about his own related experiences:
Have you ever been lost?
What was it like?
What did you do?

Link with next picture

The link with the next picture should centre on where the man will take black kitten:
I wonder where the man will take black kitten now?
Where do you think the man will go now?
Might he take black kitten home?

Black kitten gets lost   4

Picture 5

Central meaning

This contains the following ideas:
The man has brought the kitten home to his family and all the children are pleased to see him.

Opening questions

Now what has happened?
Where's the black kitten got to now?

Follow-up questions

1 If the child does not recognize that the kitten has been brought home to the family, then the teacher might help him to interpret the picture by asking:
What is the man doing here?
Where has the man brought the kitten? Is it his home?
What are the children doing?
2 If and when the child recognizes the central meaning, then the reason for the children's excitement would be explored.
Are the children pleased to see kitten?
How do you know they're pleased?
This can lead on to help the child show his ability to reason.

Reasoning

Why do you think the man brought the kitten home?
Why do you think the children are pleased?
Do you think mother is pleased? Why? or Why not?

Projecting

What do you think black kitten is thinking now?
What do you think the mother will say?
What do you think the father is saying to the children?

Predicting

What might the children do now?
What might father do next?

Associated discussion

What would you say if someone brought a lost kitten to your home? What would you do with the kitten? Why would you like to have a kitten?

Link with next picture

Do you think the family will keep black kitten?
I wonder what will happen now?
Do you think black kitten will stay with the children?

Black kitten gets lost   5

Picture 6

Central meaning

This contains the following ideas:
The family (including the kitten) are having dinner.
The lady who lost the kitten is looking for him.

Opening questions

Now what is happening here?
Now what is everybody doing here?

Follow-up questions

1 If the child is not able to abstract the overall meaning for this picture, he can be helped by questions like the following:
What is the little kitten doing now?
What are the children doing?
What is the mother doing?
What is the lady (coming up the path) doing do you think?
2 If the child indicates that he is aware of the central meaning, then the reasons for his statements can be explored.

Reasoning

Do you think the family will want to keep the kitten?
Why do you think that?
Why has the lady who lost the kitten come?

Projecting

What do you think little black kitten is thinking now?
What has the mother been doing?
What is the little girl thinking?
What is the boy thinking?
What is father thinking now?
What is the lady outside thinking?
What will she say to the family?
What will she say to black kitten?
What do you think the black kitten will want to do now?
Why do you think that?

Predicting

What will the lady who lost the kitten do now?
What will happen next?

Associated discussion

How would you look after a kitten if you had one?
What kind of things do kittens like most of all?
What should you do if you find a kitten?

The teacher will then want to help the child find a satisfactory ending for the story, whether black kitten stays or goes home with the lady, whichever the child feels is best.

Black kitten gets lost 6

Dad forgets his dinner

Picture 1

Central meaning

The child should be helped to extract a central meaning containing the following ideas:

Dad has set off to work and has forgotten the sandwiches mother was getting ready for his dinner. The boy is trying to tell dad to come back.

Opening questions

What do you think has happened here?
I wonder what's happening here?

Follow-up questions

1 If the child shows he is not aware of the central meaning and starts by labelling or describing what each person is doing, then the teacher can draw his attention to the features that provide the essential meaning. For example, if the child has not made the connection between the man in the distance and the sandwiches on the table, then attention can be focussed on this, using questions like:

Look, dad's hurrying to work
Why do you think mother is looking like that?
Who do you think the sandwiches are for?
What might have happened?

2 If the child indicates that he has grasped the central meaning, then questions could try to help him reason further.

Reasoning

Why has mother been making sandwiches?

Why does dad take sandwiches with him?
Why can't the boy make dad hear?
Why can't the boy run and catch dad quickly?

Projecting

The child might be asked what the mother is thinking or saying and what the children might decide to do next:

What do you think the mother is saying?
What will dad think when he finds he's forgotten his sandwiches?
What do you think the girl is saying to her mother?
What do you think the boy is shouting?

Predicting

What will the children do now?
How can they catch dad?

Associated discussions

Some children may already have recognized the kind of building the children live in or may have questioned why the man (dad) looks so little. Others may need encouragement to recognize that the family are in a flat:

What kind of house do they live in?
Is it like yours?
or
Is Dad really a very little man, do you think?
Why not?
Why does he look so small?

Link with next picture

What do you think will happen now?
What might the children do now?

Dad forgets his dinner 1

Picture 2

Central meaning

The child should be helped to establish a central meaning—containing the following ideas:

The children are trying to cross a busy main road; the girl is afraid her brother will step into the road before the traffic stops.

Opening questions

What's happening to the children now?
What is happening now?
What's going on here I wonder?

Follow-up questions

1   If the child fails to see the central meaning and does not recognize the danger, the teacher can direct his attention to the little girl:

Why is the girl trying to stop the boy?
Why is she holding him back?
Is it safe to cross here? Why?

2   If the child recognizes the central meaning, the teacher can try to help him reason further.

Reasoning

What should the children do now? Why?

How do the children know what to do?
Why should you be careful whenever you cross the road?

Projecting

What is the girl thinking?
What is the boy thinking?
Why is the boy trying to hurry?

Predicting

What will happen now?
What will the boy do?
What will the bus driver do next?

Associated discussion

The child might like to tell how he comes to school. Does he cross busy roads? How does he do this?

How do you come to school?
Why must we be careful on busy roads?
What makes streets dangerous?

Link with next picture

The children haven't found their dad yet have they? I wonder what they'll do now.

Dad forgets his dinner 2

Picture 3

Central meaning

This contains the following ideas:
The children go through the park and they would like to stop but there isn't time.

Opening questions

What is happening now?
What are they doing now?

Follow-up questions

1 If the child only mentions that they are in the park or playground and does not recognize the central meaning, his attention can be drawn to the children's expressions:
Do you think the children have time to play in the park now? Why not?
Why haven't the children time to play in the park just now?

2 If the child recognizes that the boy is calling to his sister not to stop and play, further questions can ask him how he knows this, and ask for the reason.

Reasoning

Why doesn't the brother want to let his sister stop and play?
Why must they hurry on?

Projecting

What do you think the boy is shouting?
What do you think the little girl is thinking?

Associated discussion

The park setting may encourage the child to recall his own visits to parks or playgrounds. He could describe and compare his own park and tell what he likes to do best in a park.

Link with next picture

Where are the children going? Do you remember?
I wonder how much further the children must go before they find their father.

Dad forgets his dinner 3

Picture 4

Central meaning

This contains the following ideas:
The children have come to the building-site and see their father is at work on a building.

Opening questions

What is happening now?
What do you think the children are doing here?

Follow-up questions

1   If the child does not recognize that the picture is of a building-site or that the man working on the building is father, then follow-up questions should try to establish this:
Where are the children now?
Who do you think the man might be?
What is father doing?
2   If the child recognizes the central meaning of the picture and establishes father as the house builder, then questions can aim at helping the child to think about the picture.

Reasoning

What work does father do? How can you tell?
Is father a little man? Why does he look so little?
Can the children give the sandwiches to dad? Why not?

How would they do that?
How can the children get the dinner to dad?

Projecting

What do you think the children are thinking?
What do you think the boy will say to his dad?
What do you think dad will say to the children?
What might the boy say to his sister?
What do you think it would feel like to be where dad is?
What would you be able to see from there?

Associated discussion

The child might remember going to see his father at his work place, or he might talk about what his father's job is. He might recall a building-site near his home and what is going on there and the kinds of jobs that builders do in a house. It is important not to let the child digress too much from the subject of the picture.

Link with next picture

Attention should be focussed on the problem of getting the dinner to dad. How might dad get his dinner?—a consideration of possibilities, e.g. coming down the ladder, using the bucket, leaving his dinner somewhere safe in the house. The child might be asked to predict what will happen and then turn to next page to see if he is right.

Dad forgets his dinner 4

Picture 5

Central meaning

This contains the following ideas:
The children are putting dad's dinner into a bucket and dad is going to pull it up.

Opening questions

Were you right?
What are the children doing?

Follow-up questions

1   If the child does not realize what the children are doing, the teacher could ask:
What are the children doing now?
How can they get the sandwiches to dad?
What do you think Dad is going to do?
What are they doing with the bucket?
Can dad get his sandwiches from the bucket now?
2   If the child recognizes the central meaning, the discussion can then centre on the problem:
Is that a good idea?
Will it work?
Could they get the sandwiches to dad in another way?
Once the central meaning is established the child can be stimulated to think in other ways.

Reasoning

Why is using the bucket a good idea?

What would dad have done if the children hadn't taken his dinner?
Will the children be pleased they've found dad? Why?

Projecting

The building-site picture offers an opportunity for the child to project into the excitement of the children loading the bucket:
What is dad saying?
What are the children saying?
How else could dad have got his sandwiches?

Associated discussion

The child might be led to talk about how houses are built and why the scaffolding is needed. What kind of materials are needed for building houses?
Why do builders need to put up a scaffold like this when they are building?
How do builders get the bricks up to where they are building?

Link with next picture

Now that dad's got his dinner what will the children do?
What will dad tell them to do?
Look and see what happened.

Dad forgets his dinner 5

Picture 6

Central meaning

This contains the following ideas:
The children have run home and their mother has something nice to eat ready for them.

Opening questions

What is happening now, do you think?

Follow-up questions

1   If the child does not see the children have now run home, the teacher could help him by asking:
Where are the children now?
Do you think this is their home? How do you know?
What is mother doing, do you think?
2   When the central meaning has been established the child can be helped to think further.

Reasoning

Are they tired now? Why?
Why have they been running?
Why has mother got the lemonade out for them?
Is mother pleased with the children? Why?

Projecting

The picture encourages the child to identify with the children's eagerness to get home again and the welcome they get from their mother.
What do you think the children are thinking?
What will they tell mum about their adventure?
What is mum saying to them?
What do you think mum is saying to the children?

Associated discussion

This might dwell on any experience the child has had of going anywhere without his own mother, and his feelings about it; or the teacher might return to the setting of the story in a flat in a tall building and ask the child to compare it with his own home. How are a house and a flat different? Or he could talk about going home.
What do you like to eat when you get home?
Do you ever run errands for your mother? Where?
What do you do then?
After discussing this final picture the teacher could briefly summarize the whole story, to ensure that the child has followed the story line from picture to picture, and finishes with an understanding of what has happened.

Dad forgets his dinner 6

Bibliography

AXLINE, V. (1964) *Dibs in Search of Self* Penguin

BERNSTEIN, B. (1971, 1973) *Class, Codes and Control Volumes* 1 *and* 2 Routledge and Kegan Paul

FURTH, H. G. (1966) *Thinking without Language* Collier Macmillan

INHELDER, B. and PIAGET, J. (1964) *The Early Growth of Logic in the Child* Routledge and Kegan Paul

LEWIS, M. M. (1968) *Language and Personality in Deaf Children* NFER

LEWIS, M. M. (1969) *Language and the Child* NFER

PARRY, M. (1975) *Preschool Education* (Schools Council Research Studies) Macmillan

PARRY, M. and ARCHER, H. (1975) *Two to Five* (Schools Council Preschool Education Project (2–5) Macmillan

TOUGH, J. (1974) *Focus on Meaning* Allen and Unwin

TOUGH, J. (1977) *The Development of Meaning: A Study of Children's Use of Language* Allen and Unwin

TOUGH, J. (in preparation) *Talking and Learning: A Guide to Fostering Communication Skills in Nursery and Infant Schools* Ward Lock Educational

VYGOTSKY, L. S. (1962) *Thought and Language* New York: Wiley

WILKINSON, A. M. (1971) *The Foundations of Language* Oxford University Press

Index

Communication Skills Workshop (Stage 1 Appraisal)

Six twenty-minute video tapes, a *Workshop Leader's Handbook* and *Workshop Members' Worksheets*, together with *Listening to Children Talking*, form the basis for workshop sessions for groups of teachers.

Video tapes

The video tapes are available from Drake Educational Associates. They can be supplied in a range of different formats and it is important when ordering to state clearly the make, series and model number of the video tape recorder on which the tapes are to be used. For free technical advice on compatibility of tapes, please write direct to Drake Educational Associates.

Tape 1 The Development of Language
Tape 2 Observing Children
Tape 3 Communication Difficulties
Tape 4 Children's Use of Language
Tape 5 Using the Picture Books
Tape 6 Making Appraisals in the Classroom

Workshop Leader's Handbook

The *Handbook* is designed to help those who wish to organize a series of workshop sessions for groups of teachers. It gives advice about how to organize the sessions and using the video tapes as a basis for discussion and practical work.

ISBN 0 7062 3611 4 £3.00 net

Workshop Members' Worksheets

The *Worksheets* include lists of questions, transcriptions of the video tapes, observation schedules or supplementary examples of children's talk. The six sets of worksheets correspond to the six video tapes. The worksheets are supplied in packs of twenty.

Topic 1 The Development of Language
ISBN 0 7062 3613 0 **20p net**
Topic 2 Observing Children
ISBN 0 7062 3614 9 **20p net**
Topic 3 Communication Difficulties
Part 1: The Quiet Child
ISBN 0 7062 3615 7 **20p net**
Part 2: Communication Difficulties
ISBN 0 7062 3612 2 **20p net**
Topic 4 Children's Use of Language
ISBN 0 7062 3616 5 **20p net**
Topic 5 Using the Picture Books
ISBN 0 7062 3617 3 **20p net**
Topic 6 Making Appraisals in the Classroom
ISBN 0 7062 3618 1 **20p net**

The video tapes, *Leader's Handbook* and *Members' Worksheets* are all available from Drake Educational Associates. The *Leader's Handbook* and *Members' Worksheets* are also available from Ward Lock Educational.

Drake Educational Associates
212 Whitchurch Road
Cardiff CF4 3XF   Tel. Cardiff 29414
Ward Lock Educational
116 Baker Street
London W1M 2BB   Tel. 01 486 3271